A Contrastive Phonology of Portuguese and English

Milton M. Azevedo

Georgetown University Press, Washington, D.C. 20057

Library of Congress Cataloging in Publication Data

Azevedo, Milton Mariano, 1942-
A contrastive phonology of Portuguese and English.

1. Portuguese language--Phonology. 2. English language--Phonology. 3. Portuguese language--Grammar, Comparative--English. 4. English language--Grammar, Comparative--Portuguese. I. Title.
PC5076.A97 469.1'5 81-4392
ISBN 0-87840-082-6 AACR2

Printed in the United States of America

International Standard Book Number: 0-87840-082-6

Ao Francisco Gomes de Matos,
colega e amigo.

CONTENTS

1

INTRODUCTION

1.1 Introduction. This monograph is intended as a contrastive study of select aspects of the phonological systems of English and Portuguese. The dialects chosen for comparison are General American English and the variety of Portuguese spoken in Southeastern Brazil. As regards the latter, primary reference is made to the Paulista dialect of the city of São Paulo, complemented by comments, whenever appropriate, on the dialects of the cities of Rio de Janeiro (Carioca) and Belo Horizonte (Mineiro). Sources have included published descriptions of the phonology of either language such as are listed in the References and data from field work done in Brazil in the summer of 1977.

This study follows the line of linguistic inquiry represented by works such as those of Moulton (1962), Agard and Di Pietro (1965), Stockwell and Bowen (1965), and Kufner (1971). Like most contrastive analyses, it takes a directional approach, in which English is considered the source language (L-1) and Portuguese the target language (L-2). Similarities and differences between the two languages are viewed within the general frame of reference of the acquisition of the phonological system of L-2 by a native speaker of L-1. It is expected that the findings presented should have some pedagogical relevance and that, as such, they should be of interest not only to applied linguists but also to teachers and advanced students of Portuguese. However, this book is neither a pronunciation manual nor a protocol for direct application of the techniques of contrastive analysis to the teaching of Portuguese as a foreign language. Rather, it is conceived as a study in a specific area of applied linguistics, namely the application of phonological analysis to the contrasting of two languages for the primary purpose of ascertaining which phonological traits are shared by them and which are found in one but not the other.

1.2 Phonological description. A contrastive phonological analysis involves the comparison of the sound systems of L-1 and L-2 or, to put it more accurately, of the linguistic representations of those systems. Since the linguist does not have direct access to the systems themselves, he must work with theoretical constructs which he accepts as descriptions of the systems. Such descriptions may be more or less abstract, depending on the proximity which obtains between those constructs and surface phonological phenomena.

Like descriptive phonology, so also contrastive phonological analysis can be carried out at different degrees of abstractness. What constitutes the optimum degree of abstractness in phonology has been a topic of debate for some time, and there is indication of a tendency in favor of representations that are far more concrete--that is, closer to surface phonetics--than would have been acceptable to many a phonologist a decade or so ago.[1]

Unlike descriptive phonology, contrastive phonology, if it is to be more than an intellectual game, cannot be satisfied with having as its point of reference an ideal speaker-listener for the analysis of whose linguistic competence abstract phonology suffices. Rather, it must take into account that, for a flesh-and-blood speaker of L-1, the only means of access to L-2 are its surface forms, which he must compare with the surface forms of his native L-1. The input to his auditory perception are the actual sounds of L-2, not their phonological representations in terms of rules, autonomous or systematic phonemes, and the like.

According to a hypothesis of second language acquisition, the learner initially processes and interprets those sounds in terms of his own phonological system. When he attempts to speak L-2, he resorts to approximations of those sounds based on his interpretation, and consequently the phonetics of his rendering of L-2 will contain features of L-1. Acquisition of correct--that is, native-like--phonological competence in L-2 requires the development of the ability both to recognize and produce L-2 sounds and their combinations. That ability results from the learner's building for himself a replica of the phonological system of L-2, an activity at the level labeled by Kohler (1971:87) as 'the level of articulatory control and auditory perception in all its gradations.'

Several aspects of that activity are relevant for a contrastive analysis. At the very minimum, the learner must become able to discriminate among the individual sounds of L-2 and to distinguish them from L-1 sounds; he also has to learn to articulate L-2 sounds and their combinations; and he must internalize the relationships among the sounds of L-2, that is, the phonological rules which hold them together as a system.

In developing for himself a replica of L-2, the learner goes through a process of successive approximations, the result of which is a series of phonological systems, each progressively closer to that of L-2. Those systems make up what has been called an interlanguage, that is, the learner's own variety of

L-2.[2] In putting together the phonology of this interlanguage, he utilizes not only raw phonetic data acquired through direct contact with speakers of L-2 but also explicit information available to him on the phonology of L-2, besides rules borrowed from his native L-1, and presumably whatever his own faculté de langage tells him about what a phonological system should be like. The resulting system may be viewed as a set of working hypotheses to be tested in his attempts to speak L-2. This is an unstable, changing system, always subject to rectification. Some hypotheses are found adequate and retained permanently--as when an English speaker finds out that the initial sound of ship [šɩp] can be used successfully in the pronunciation of Portuguese words like chato ['šatu] and caixa ['kayšə], for example. Other hypotheses are expanded into more general ones, as when a learner of English discovers that there is an aspiration rule that applies to all voiceless stops in initial position. There are also hypotheses which are dropped as inappropriate, as when a speaker of Portuguese learning English finds out that the sounds [iy] and [ɩ] cannot be used interchangeably in stressed position, since they signal minimal contrasts, as in leap [liyp] vs. lip [lɩp].

This view of language acquisition implies an interplay between the phonological system of L-1 and that of L-2, the result of which is an intermediary system which, if all goes well, evolves toward a replica of L-2, as the learner discovers 'how the speaker of the target language perceptually organizes the range of sounds he makes and hears into groups, and which distinctive features he pays attention to' (Corder 1973:248). It also implies that it is the surface phonetic representation of L-1 that constitutes a model or input for the learner. A consequence of those implications is that they suggest that the phonological representation used in a contrastive analysis should closely approximate the phonetic representation of what is perceived by the learner. According to Corder (1973:250),

> whatever phonological theoretical approach we adopt ... it is only in terms of the actual physical output of sounds, i.e. the physiological-acoustic terms, that we can make rigorous comparisons ... this is where 'idealization' comes in again. We have to set up an 'inventory' of 'norms' which represent some abstraction from the actual data of speech and treat these as the 'sounds of the language'.

This study concerns itself only with matters of phonetics and phonology, and does not take into account morphological problems of the type found in works such as, for example, Harris (1969), Mateus (1975), or Cressey (1978). One of the reasons for this limitation of scope lies in the adopted focus on the acquisition of the sound system of L-2 by a speaker of L-1. There is little reason to believe that this process, in and by itself, involves the acquisition of morphology beyond the rules of phonotactics governing the possible arrangements of phonemes and phenomena such as liaison, synalepha, and the like. Nor is there reason to assume that, for the learner of L-2, acquisition of its phonology somehow depends on acquisition of syntax. It is possible to acquire control over the phonology of a foreign language while remaining rather ignorant of the rules underlying the syntactic representation of its utterances. Opera singers who sing in languages they cannot speak and comedians who can put together whole strings of nonsense sound sequences in a foreign language, without any attempt at producing grammatical utterances, are two extreme examples which illustrate this possibility. Admittedly, most learners go about it the other way around, that is, they usually develop a more limited control of the phonology than of the grammar and vocabulary of the target language. This, however, is a consequence of their goals, since the ability to communicate, even with an obvious foreign accent, tends to be prized over native-like pronunciation which is accompanied by limited means of expression. Thus it is not surprising that most foreign-language courses pay far more attention to grammar and vocabulary than to phonology, as evidenced by the scant space usually devoted to pronunciation in most school manuals.

The focus on phonology adopted here, although diverging from the models of language based on one or another version of generative grammar, is compatible with more flexible models, such as the one proposed by Leech (1974), in which semantics, syntax, and phonology each constitutes a separate autonomous component with its own rules and well-formedness conditions. The possibility of thus keeping phonology apart from the other components of a theoretical model is one of the assumptions about the nature of language underlying this study. Another assumption is that since the input to the foreign language learner is provided by surface phonetic forms, it is at the surface level that the analyst should seek the relevant contrasts, many of which can be stated in terms very much like those found in traditional phonemic analysis. Time and again it has been pointed out by linguists of different persuasions that the notion of phoneme has a role to play in phonological description (Wang 1968, Schane 1971, O'Connor 1973). The usefulness of the phoneme in contrastive phonology, in both its theoretical and its practical aspects, lends credence to those claims.

One or two examples suffice to illustrate this point. Chomsky and Halle (1968) have shown that underlying tense vowels may be postulated as the source of both surface diphthongs and simple vowels for at least some dialects of modern English. This information, however, is of limited use for the foreign learner of English, for whom what counts is the surface manifestation of complex syllable nuclei and their contrast in English with simple nuclei (as in <u>my</u> [may] vs. <u>Ma</u> [ma], or <u>bait</u> [beyt] vs. <u>bet</u> [bɛt]), or with Portuguese syllable nuclei (as in Eng. lay [ley] vs. Ptg. lê [le], or Eng. see [siy] vs. Ptg. si [si]). Likewise, even if it can be proved beyond doubt that stress is predictable in both languages from a generative viewpoint, this information is of but limited value to a learner of English who must learn as a new item each of the contrasts represented by pairs such as 'permit (n.) vs. per'mit (v.), 'conduct (n.) vs. con'duct (v.), etc.[3]

The need for phonological representations capable of capturing contrasts operative at the surface level has led to the decision to avoid the abstractness typical of works in generative phonology and work instead with surface contrasts such as are dealt with in the contrastive works mentioned in Section 1.1.[4] In the brief phonological account of Portuguese (Chapter 2) and English (Chapter 3), surface contrasts are related to underlying phonemes which are characterized in terms of distinctive features. Certain contrasts, such as the higher mid vowels ([e], [o]) vs. the lower mid ones ([ɛ], [ɔ]) in Portuguese, are shown as obtaining in the underlying representation as well. Others, such as the nasal vs. oral vowels in Portuguese, are considered surface phenomena resulting from the application of specific phonological rules to underlying phonemes.

As Corder points out (1973:248f.), a contrastive phonological analysis operates at two separate and yet interdependent levels. At one level, it deals with articulatory and acoustic matters, such as how the initial sound in Eng. tap is like (or unlike) the initial sound in Ptg. tapa, and so on. This type of comparison focuses largely on articulatory phonetic details (such as the position of the articulators, the degree of nasalization, or the timing of vibration of the vocal cords). Also at this level is the comparison of specific processes considered in isolation, such as the conditions for nasalization of vowels and their consequences, for example.

The other level of analysis involves comparison of the ways the sounds of each language interact with one another in a consistent system. At this functional level, the system operates as a self-contained entity in which each part depends, for its characterization, on its relationship with the other parts. Since the number of parts of the system of L-1, their individual phonological characterization, and the relationships among them do not necessarily have symmetric homologues in the system of L-2, intersystem comparison at the functional level is necessarily approximative:

> ... phonemes having the same label in two languages ... are generally realized by sounds which have some acoustic and articulatory characteristics in common, but this does not mean that they are otherwise comparable (Corder 1973: 249).

The forms used for contrastive purposes are in most cases surface or near-to-surface representations, and the phonological transcriptions used should be regarded as a kind of notational shorthand intended to facilitate the analysis by omitting irrelevant details. The unit phonemes of those transcriptions are functional abstractions rather than self-contained units in the traditional structuralist sense. The resources of generative phonology have also been used here to highlight processes and relationships relevant for the contrastive analysis. This means the approach adopted is eclectic--enlightenedly so, one would hope--but apologies do not seem necessary on this score. Applied linguistics is a field of research in (among other things) the application of theories to concrete problems. In the present case, the problem is the comparison of two phonological systems from the viewpoint of the problems faced by a speaker of L-1 about to acquire L-2, and the analyst has to choose those aspects of available theories which best lend themselves to the description and explanation of the phenomena upon which he wishes to focus.

1.3 Contrastive analysis and foreign language acquisition. The criticism directed against contrastive analysis over the last decade or so has not shaken the conviction held by many linguists that contrastive studies can contribute to illuminating similarities and differences between languages. This is certainly not a minor contribution, since comparison of different languages is a means of providing an empirical basis for generalizations about language. Contrastive analysis can also contribute to an understanding of the problems of acquisition of a foreign language and, indirectly, to the preparation of linguistically sound teaching materials.[5] That much of the criticism referred to has been misdirected has already been shown by James (1971) in his refutation of Lee (1968). Nevertheless, the theory and practice of contrastive analysis have changed over the years, and some of its initial claims have been supplanted by a more limited view of what it can and should try to accomplish. This is particularly the case with regard to the so-called 'strong hypothesis' (Wardhaugh 1970), according to which a thorough contrastive analysis would make it possible to predict the errors which speakers of L-1 tend to make when acquiring L-2. Both the scope of the original claim to predictive value and its critique were magnified out of proportion in the general upheaval of linguistic theory in the sixties. In fact, from the very inception of contrastive studies serious practitioners viewed error prediction in statistic, that is, probabilistic, rather than absolute terms, as shown in the following statement by Lado (1968:124-125).

> From these contrastive studies we have been able to predict probabilistically many of the distortions that a speaker of L-1 is most likely to introduce into L-2 as he learns it ...

> the inventory of distortions does not represent behavior that will be exhibited by every subject on every trial. It represents behavior that is likely to appear with greater than random frequency, and it represents pressures that have to be overcome.

Contrastive phonology highlights similarities and differences between specific aspects of the sound systems of two or more languages. Even if its predictive value is only statistical (as is, in fact, the value of scientific prediction in general), it makes it possible to explain, in a principled and systematic way, learners' errors which can be ascribed to negative transfer of phonological features of L-1 to their version of L-2.

By focusing on those similarities and differences between the two sound systems, contrastive phonology makes it possible to set up scales of structural divergence between the two systems. Such scales serve to determine which features of L-1 can be directly transferred to L-2, which features of L-2 have no counterpart in L-1, and so on. However, it seems preferable to speak of a scale of structural divergence, rather than of 'hierarchical difficulty' (Stockwell and Bowen 1965:13ff.). The reason is that the latter expression appears to imply a degree of certainty about what constitutes difficulty for the learner that cannot be supported on the basis of contrastive analysis alone. However, contrastive linguistics does not go into questions such as the psychological factors involved in foreign language acquisition which would be required to substantiate claims about the relative difficulty posed by varying degrees of divergence between L-1 and L-2.

1.4 Acknowledgments. I wish to thank Professor Frederick B. Agard (emeritus, Cornell University) for a fruitful exchange of ideas prior to and during the writing of this book, and Professors Jerry Craddock (University of California, Berkeley) and Cléa Rameh (Georgetown University) for their invaluable comments on the manuscript. It goes without saying that I alone am responsible for any extant imperfections. Thanks are also extended to several anonymous speakers of Portuguese and English who acted as informants and to Ms. Florence C. Myer of El Cerrito, California, for the patience and expertise with which she turned the erratic original into readable typescript. A special word of appreciation goes to Richard J. O'Brien, S.J., General Editor and Director of Georgetown University Press, for his constant interest and encouragement.

This study was made possible by a grant-in-aid for field work in Brazil provided by The Tinker Foundation through the Center for Latin American Studies of the University of California, Berkeley, and by a one-quarter sabbatical leave granted by the latter institution, both of which are gratefully acknowledged.

NOTES

1. The most important movement in this direction is natural generative phonology. See Hooper (1976) and Venneman (1974a,b).

2. On interlanguage, a.k.a. transitional competence, see Corder (1967, 1971, 1973, 1975); Hanzeli (1975); Nemser (1971); and Selinker (1972).

3. Such contrasts are susceptible of systematic treatment under any of several theoretical approaches, as shown by Householder (1971). For the learner, however, unless he be a trained linguist, such analyses are of scant value, at least in the initial stages of his training.

4. Corder (1973:252) remarks that although the generative approach 'holds out better hopes of descriptive adequacy ... and accords with some of the recent theories of how languages are learned ... it does not, because of the problem of common categories, lend itself readily to comparative techniques.'

5. A recent instance of this application of contrastive analysis is Terrell and Salgués (1979).

6. Examples of English interference in Portuguese were obtained from recordings made by students at the University of California, Berkeley--referred to in subsequent chapters as 'subjects'.

2

THE SOUNDS OF PORTUGUESE

2.1 **Introduction.** This chapter presents an analysis of the main characteristics of Portuguese sounds from two complementary viewpoints, namely, their phonetic features and the way in which those sounds operate together as a system. The latter viewpoint presupposes, in turn, two modes of analysis. The first mode aims at determining a finite inventory of phonological primes, or phonemes, understood as sets of distinctive features such that each set contrasts with all others. The second mode takes into account the fact that, when phonemes are combined in meaningful sequences, they interact with one another, in processes describable by means of phonological rules. Such processes act upon the feature specification of the phonemes, originating subphonemic or allophonic variations of the latter and determining the phonetic characteristics of the output actualized in speech.

2.2 **Vowels.** In the articulation of vowels, the airstream coming from the lungs passes through the oral cavity without encountering any stricture of the articulators or obstacles capable of forming a consonant sound. As opposed to consonants and glides, vowels can be prolonged indefinitely, as long as egressive lung air is available, but otherwise there are enough similarities among these sound types to make it possible to classify them according to the same parameters, by means of a system of distinctive features. Nevertheless, it is traditional to classify vowels by taking into account as primary parameters the shape and position of the tongue and the shape of the lips. Features such as the presence or absence of nasality or voicing, for example, constitute secondary parameters which allow for a more detailed classification.

The shape and position of the tongue can be determined by reference to a system of two orthogonal axes, so as to plot a series of positions, each corresponding to a phonetically distinct vowel. The points on the vertical axis correspond to the height of the tongue, that is, the vertical position of its

Figure 2.1 Cardinal vowels.

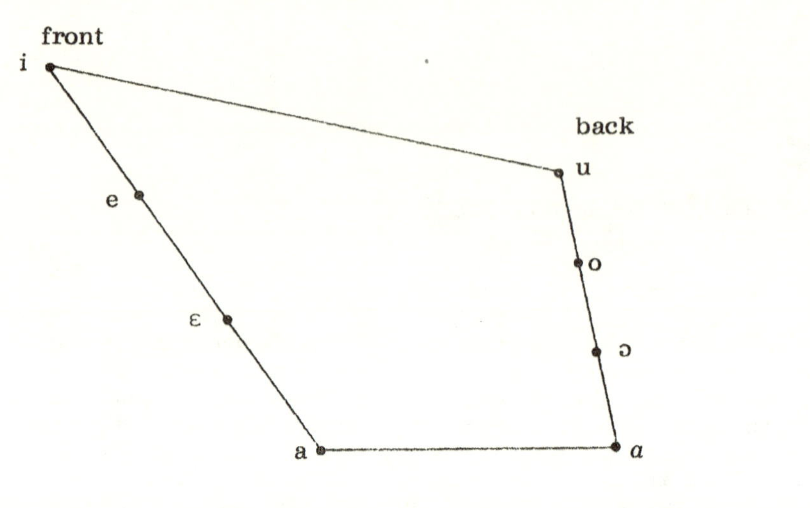

Figure 2.2 Articulatory classification of Portuguese vowels.

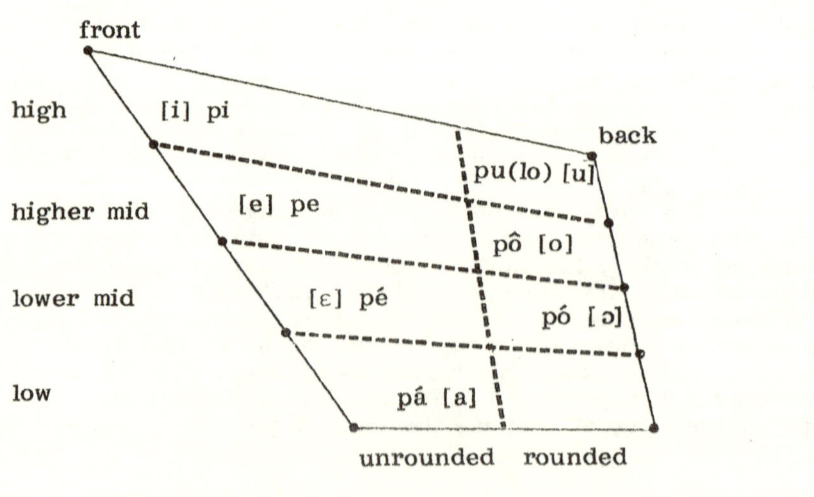

highest portion. This dimension allows for the classification of vowels along a continuum from lowest to highest. The points on the horizontal axis, in turn, correspond to the degree of fronting of the tongue. This dimension makes it possible to classify vowels along a continuum ranging from back to front.

Since each axis stands for a line of continuous displacement, an indeterminate number of intermediary positions are theoretically possible, each corresponding to a combination of different degrees of tongue height or fronting. A small subset of that indeterminate number suffices for establishing the vowel phonemes. These vowels are classified by reference to the system of cardinal vowels (after Jones 1956:36) shown in Figure 2.1, and they correspond to the phonetic vowels which occur in stressed position, as in pi, pe, pé, pá, pó, pô, and pu (Figure 2.2).

Regarding the height dimension, a four-point system suffices to classify Portuguese vowels as high, higher mid, lower mid, and low; and as to the horizontal position of that organ, a three-point system is enough to characterize them as front, central, and back. The shape of the lips, which varies from very rounded to rather spread, is a concomitant feature in the articulation of vowels in any given position defined by those parameters. It is clear from Figure 2.2 that lip-rounding accompanies the articulation of back vowels and is absent in the formation of nonback ones, and is consequently a redundant classificatory feature. Furthermore, if a binary system is adopted in which each vowel is characterized by the presence or absence of a feature, the height dimension may be reduced from four to three points. The vowel [a] is thus sufficiently distinguished from the others as being the only central one (that is, [-front], [-back]) and the lower mid vowels [ɛ] and [ɔ] are distinguished from their respective higher mid counterparts, [e] and [o], by the feature [+low]. Such distribution of distinctive features allows the characterization of vowels shown in Figure 2.3.

Figure 2.3 Distinctive features of Portuguese vowel phonemes.

	/i	e	ɛ	a	ɔ	o	u/
[high]	+	–	–	–	–	–	+
[low]	–	–	+	+	+	–	–
[front]	+	+	+	–	–	–	–
[back]	–	–	–	–	+	+	+

Additional features differentiate the vowels from other elements in the sound system. Vowels are distinguished from consonants by the minus value of the feature [consonantal], which refers to the presence of an obstruction in the oral cavity, typical of the articulation of consonants in general.

If, during the production of a sound, the velum is lowered, part of the egressive lung air voiced by the glottis escapes through the nasal cavity which, functioning as a resonance chamber, imparts to the sound a quality described by the feature [+nasal]. All of the vowels in Figure 2.3 are [-nasal], thus differing from the [+nasal] vowels of words like sim [sĩ], lã [lə̃], som [sõ], um [ũ], etc.

The vowels in Figure 2.3 are also produced with simultaneous vibration of the vocal cords, and they are thus marked [+voiced], to distinguish them from their [-voiced] nondistinctive (that is, allophonic) counterparts. The possibility of spontaneous vibration of the vocal cords during the production of a sound corresponds to the feature [+sonorant], which vowels share with glides as well as liquid and lateral consonants. Finally, vowels are all [+syllabic], that is, they can be the nucleus of a syllable. This feature distinguishes them not only from consonants, which are all [-syllabic], but also from the glides [w] and [y], which appear in diphthongs and triphthongs (Section 2.4). Figure 2.4 shows the complete classification of the vowel phonemes postulated in this study.

Figure 2.4 Feature specification of Portuguese vowel phonemes.

	/i	e	ɛ	a	ɔ	o	u/
[consonantal]	–	–	–	–	–	–	–
[sonorant]	+	+	+	+	+	+	+
[syllabic]	+	+	+	+	+	+	+
[high]	+	–	–	–	–	–	+
[low]	–	–	+	+	+	–	–
[front]	+	+	+	–	–	–	–
[back]	–	–	–	–	+	+	+
[nasal]	–	–	–	–	–	–	–
[voiced]	+	+	+	+	+	+	+
[rounded]	–	–	–	–	+	+	+

2.3 Vowel reduction. The system shown in Figure 2.3 corresponds to maximum contrast among vowels in stressed position. In Portuguese, as in other Romance languages, some of those oppositions are neutralized under weak stress and the vowel inventory consequently is reduced (Pottier 1967).

2.3.1 The lower mid vowels. The contrasts signalled by the two degrees of opening of mid vowels are rendered phonologically inoperative in unstressed position. Nevertheless, as shown in the examples in (2.1a), taken from Houaiss (1959: 25ff.), the vowels [ɛ] and [ɔ] can appear in pretonic position in (a) derived forms; (b) adverbs in -mente;[1] (c) certain prefixes; compound nouns involving duplication of a basic form, usually a verb, as in (d), or a sequence of verb, a connector, and a noun, or a verb, or an adverb, as in (e); and (f) a handful of hypocorisms formed by duplication of a stressed syllable with either vowel.

(2.1a)

	/ɛ/	/ɔ/
(a)	cafezinho	modinha
	papelzinho	sozinho
(b)	alegremente	somente
	corretamente	pobremente
(c)	pré-história	pré-democrático
(d)	pega-pega	troca-troca
	quero-quero	corre-corre
	lero-lero	
(e)	leva-e-traz	bota-fora
	pega-pra-capar	Botafogo
(f)	Lelé	Totó
	Teté	vovó
	Bebé	Loló

There is a general tendency for /ɛ/ and /ɔ/ to be actualized respectively as [e] and [o], as the compound nature of a given item is masked, as it were, by a higher degree of lexicalization, which imparts to the word a higher degree of phonological unity. This is noticeable in cafezinho [kafe'zĩñu] or sozinho [so'zĩñu], which in turn may become [kafi'zĩñu] and [su'zĩñu], particularly in Carioca (Houaiss 1959:26, 38) and Mineiro. In such cases, the underlying representation should show /ɛ/ of /ɔ/, and a two-part reduction rule of the general type shown in (2.1) would apply, according to variables such as the morphological type of the item, its learned or popular character, and so on.

(2.1b) $\left\{\begin{matrix} /\varepsilon/ \\ /ɔ/ \end{matrix}\right\} \rightarrow \left\{\begin{matrix} [e] \\ [o] \end{matrix}\right\}$

(2.1c) $\left\{\begin{matrix} [e] \\ [o] \end{matrix}\right\} \rightarrow \left\{\begin{matrix} [i] \\ [u] \end{matrix}\right\}$

2.3.2 Other vowels. In unstressed, nonfinal position, the remaining nonhigh vowels /a/, /e/, and /o/ undergo raising, so that the mid vowels are actualized phonetically as high (2.2a) and the low one surfaces as the mid vowel (2.2b). The exact phonetic characteristics of this last vowel vary somewhat regionally, but it is safe to describe it as [-high], [-low], [-front], and [-back].

(2.2a) $\begin{bmatrix} \text{-high} \\ \text{-low} \end{bmatrix} \rightarrow [\text{+high}]$ (2.2b) $\begin{bmatrix} \text{-high} \\ \text{+low} \\ \text{-front} \\ \text{-back} \end{bmatrix} \rightarrow [\text{-low}]$

The net effect of such raising processes is that in unstressed, nonfinal position the phonologically significant contrasts are reduced to one low vowel and four nonlow ones.

In final position, phonetic contrast is reduced to [high] vs. [low] (that is, /a/ vs. /i,u/), on the one hand, and [front] vs. [back] (that is, /i/ vs. /u/), on the other. Rule (2.2) applies regularly, although it may be blocked for reasons of emphasis, as in one possible rendering of the question: *Você disse amiga* [a'miga] *ou amigo?* [a'migo]. Phonetically, final high vowels are to be described as belonging to the types found in the range of the cardinal vowels [i] and [u]. From a phonological viewpoint, the analyst is faced with the question of which phonemes should appear in the underlying representation. Most structuralist analyses (for example, Reed and Leite 1947 or Câmara 1953) have opted for /i/ and /u/. This solution is consistent with the fact that they were concerned with standard varieties of Carioca or Paulista in which unstressed final [e] and [o] occur finally only sporadically. However, there are, within the geographical area considered in this study, certain dialects, such as Caipira,[2] in which unstressed [o] and [e] alternate finally with [u] and [i]. This was noted by Amaral (1920:22-23), who stated about the unstressed vowels:

> Na silaba pòstónica dos vocábulos graves, conservam o seu valor típico. Não se operou aqui a permuta de *e* final por *i*, que se observa em outras regiões do país (*aquêli*, *êsti*), como não se operou a de *o* por *u* (*povu*, *digu*).[3]

In a recent study of a variety of Caipira, Rodrigues (1974: 186ff.) registers several instances of varieties of final [e] and [o] in apparent free alternation with [i] and [u] in different utterances of the same lexical item, as in (2.3a), (2.3b).[4]

(2.3a) [o] ~ [u]
prego ['pṙɛgọ] ~ ['pṙɛgu]
braço ['bṙasọ] ~ ['bṙasu]
martelo [maṟ'tɛlọ] ~ [maṟ'tɛlu]
pato ['patọ] ~ ['patu]
dedo ['dedo] ~ ['dedu]
gato ['gato] ~ ['gatu]

(2.3b) [e] ~ [i]
alfinete [aṟfi'nete]
bote ['bɔte] ~ ['bɔtẹ] ~ ['bɔte̤]
chale ['šali] ~ ['šalẹ]
chicote [ši'kɔte] ~ [ši'kɔtẹ]
onze ['õze] ~ ['õzi]
parede [pa'ṟedẹ] ~ [pa'ṟedẹ] ~ [pa'ṟede]

For such dialects (as well as for standard Mineiro, Carioca, and Paulista, if certain types of emphatic pronunciation are taken into account), the description would be complicated if only /i/ and /u/ were allowed in final unstressed position. In order to account for the alternation shown in (2.3a) and (2.3b), one would have to set up an allophonic distribution such that both [i] and [e] appeared as variants of /i/, and both [u] and [o] appeared as manifestations of /u/, as in (2.3c).

(2.3c) $/i/ \rightarrow \begin{cases}[i]\\ [e]\end{cases}$ as in $/bɔti/ \rightarrow \begin{cases}['bɔti]\\ ['bɔte]\end{cases}$

$/u/ \rightarrow \begin{cases}[u]\\ [o]\end{cases}$ as in $/braso/ \rightarrow \begin{cases}['brasu]\\ ['braso]\end{cases}$

If, alternatively, one had only /i/ → [i], /u/ → [u], /e/ → [e], and /o/ → [o], that alternation would have to be explained as resulting from some process of phonological replacement, which would complicate the morphological description. It is simpler and more general to posit underlying /e/, /o/ wherever [e], [o] may occur unstressed, and /i/, /u/ in items like <u>cáqui</u>, <u>juri</u>, <u>tílburi</u>, or <u>bônus</u>, which are always pronounced with final unstressed [i], [u]. The phonetic manifestation of underlying /e/, /o/ as, respectively, [i], [u] would result from the raising Rule (2.4).

(2.4) $\begin{bmatrix}+\text{syl}\\ -\text{high}\\ -\text{low}\\ \alpha\text{back}\end{bmatrix} \rightarrow \begin{bmatrix}+\text{high}\\ \alpha\text{back}\end{bmatrix}$

In nonfinal position, the phonetic characteristics of unstressed nonlow vowels vary according to the phonological environment and differences of style, register, and dialect. A full study of how such factors condition that variation remains to be done, and in this section only the more important tendencies are indicated.

In principle, the contrast between /i/ vs. /e/ and /o/ vs. /u/ can obtain in all positions, but the general tendency is toward reduction according to Rule 2.4, particularly in speech styles associated with informal or colloquial registers. If the stressed vowel is /a/, the contrast holds rather well for /i/ vs. /e/ (as in <u>pecar</u> vs. <u>picar</u> or <u>remar</u> vs. <u>rimar</u>) and less well for /o/ vs. /u/ (as in <u>fuçar</u> vs. <u>fossar</u>, or words like <u>tomate</u>, <u>botão</u>, and <u>tostão</u>, all with unstressed [o] ~ [u]).[5] If the stressed vowel is /o/ or /e/, pretonic /e/ tends to surface as [e], as in <u>fedor</u>, <u>tenor</u>, <u>temer</u>, <u>querer</u>; pretonic /o/, in turn, tends to surface as [o] as in <u>correr</u>, <u>poder</u>, <u>horror</u>, although [u] is not uncommon, as in <u>comer</u>, <u>foder</u>, etc.

In pretonic position, insofar as surface forms are concerned, several tendencies can be noticed. Before /s/, the contrast

/o/ vs. /u/ remains (as in the near-minimal pair oscular vs. ustular), but the contrast /e/ vs. /i/ is reduced to /i/. Although this contrast remains latent and can be recovered if necessary, as in estória vs. história, estoma vs. histoma, in the ordinary language only [i] is heard (Câmara 1972:33). Noninitially, and if the stressed vowel is /a/, both contrasts hold well, as in (2.5a), but there are many examples of /e/ → [i] and /o/ → [u], as in (2.5b).

(2.5a) [o], [e] [u], [i]
bocal vs. bucal
coral vs. curral
pesar vs. pisar
pelar vs. pilar

(2.5b) [o] ~ [u]
tomate
botão
jogar

If stress falls on a mid vowel, either contrast holds best if the pretonic and the stressed vowel both have the same value for [back]; otherwise, /o/ undergoes raising more readily than /e/, as the examples in (2.5d) indicate.

(2.5c)	pretonic [e]		pretonic [e] ~ [i]
	/e-é/	tecer	pelego
		beber	remendo
		dever	rebenque
		feder	arremedo
	/e-ó/	terror	depor
		professor	Agenor
		projetor	repolho

(2.5d)	pretonic [o]		pretonic [o] ~ [u]
	/o-ó/	torpor	colosso
		bolor	fogoso
		rotor	bodoso
	/o-é/	tolher	colete (n.)
		colher (v.)	roleta (n.)
		correr	modelo (n.)
			soberbo (adj.)
			chover

Many words with pretonic [e] and [o], as in (2.5c) and (2.5d), are related paradigmatically to forms with [ɛ] and [ɔ] in that position (such as tece, bebe, aterra, professa, tolhe, corre, and so on), whereas no such relationship obtains in the case of words that show the alternation [e] ~ [i] or [o] ~ [u]. This suggests that a complete morphophonological analysis should postulate underlying forms with /ɛ/ and /ɔ/

and rules to the effect that these vowels surface as [e] and [o] in the first case. Words of the second type would have underlying forms with /e/ or /o/, and the surface forms with [i] or [u] would be accounted for as a result of a reduction rule such as (2.4).

If the stressed vowel is [+high], the general tendency is for pretonic /o/ and /e/ to be raised, as in (2.6a), as well as in derived words in which /i/ or /u/ appear unstressed, as in (2.6b).

(2.6a) gemido [ži'midu]
polido [pu'lidu]
bombinha [bũ'biña]
entulho [ĩ'tul̃u]
motivo [mu'tivu]

(2.6b) entulhar [ĩtu'l̃ar]
polidez [puli'des]
gemideira [žimi'deyrə]
motivação [mutiva'sə̃w̃]

In posttonic, nonfinal position, the contrast /e/ vs. /i/ holds rather well in formal pronunciation, but only partially in informal speech. This variation in formality determines whether or not a noun like *Águeda* will rhyme with *ácida*, or *córrego* with *código*, or whether *trôpego*, *pândego*, and *bêbedo* will have [pi], [di], or [bi] instead of [pe], [de], or [be] in the penult. Persistence of [e] is often conditioned by the learned character of a word, but this probably means less than the fact that such words are usually restricted to formal speech anyway, and thus one has *lanígero*, *úmero*, and *útero* with prefinal [e], but *mamífero* with either [e] or [i]. As to the contrast /o/ vs. /u/, it holds poorly in formal speech and vanishes altogether in informal registers. Câmara (1953:135ff., 1972:34) pointed out the existence of rhymes such as *pérola*/*cérula*/*quérula* and *estrídulo*/*ídolo*, all with prefinal [u], which he ascribed to an underlying phoneme /u/. The possibility of correctly articulating an [o], even if only in deliberate pronunciation, betrays the presence of an underlying /o/ in words like *pérola* and *ídolo*, as opposed to *trêmula* and *báculo*, which have /u/ in the underlying representation.

2.4 Diphthongs and triphthongs. In one analysis, the production of the sequences of sounds that form syllables and syllable sequences is intimately linked with respiration, whose two stages--inspiration and expiration--depend on the one hand on the movements of the abdominal muscles which support the diaphragm, and on the other on the intercostal muscles which connect the ribs. The abdominal muscles move the diaphragm vertically, increasing or decreasing the volume of the thorax, and the intercostal muscles have a similar action laterally, increasing or decreasing the space between the ribs. Coordinated action of those two movements allows the lungs to contract and expand, filling up with air or expelling it. While diaphragm movements are more or less regular during the foregoing process, those of the intercostal muscles undergo quick variations, thus producing a sequence of pulses. From a physiological viewpoint, the sequence of sounds produced during one such pulse corresponds to a syllable, whose articulation corresponds to a culminating point in expiratory muscular activity. The entire sequence of sounds produced during an expiratory movement constitutes a stress phrase, which can contain one or more syllables.

It is also possible to characterize a syllable from an acoustic viewpoint. The sounds of a given sequence differ among themselves as to sonority, on account of different ratios of vibration of the vocal cords and for other reasons, such as the amount of resonance that takes place in the pharynx, the mouth, or the nasal cavity. The variation in sonority among the sounds of a sequence can be plotted on a curve, where peaks and dips alternate regularly. The syllable can then be defined as being made up of the sounds included between two successive dips. The peak between these constitutes the nucleus of the syllable, and the sounds preceding and following the nucleus are, respectively, the onset and the coda of the syllable. The nucleus is minimally formed by a vowel, which may be accompanied by one or two glides, thus forming a diphthong or a triphthong, according to formula (2.7), in which the parentheses indicate the optional character of the glides.

(2.7) $$\$ \left(\begin{bmatrix}\text{-cons}\\ \text{-syl}\end{bmatrix}\right) \begin{bmatrix}\text{-cons}\\ \text{+syl}\end{bmatrix} \left(\begin{bmatrix}\text{-cons}\\ \text{-syl}\end{bmatrix}\right) \$$$

In general terms, the articulation of a syllable includes three stages: (1) the onset, which corresponds to the beginning of a pulse and the progressive opening of the articulators, moving from the articulation of a consonant to that of the vowel in the nucleus; (2) the peak, which corresponds to the articulation of the nucleus and presents maximum opening, intensity, and sonority; and (3) the final phase or coda, which corresponds to the end of the pulse and a progressive closure of the articulators, from the position of articulation of the vowel toward that of a semivowel or consonant. Syllables ending in a vowel or semivowel are called open, and those ending in a consonant are called closed. This general scheme may vary. If the syllable begins in a vowel, it has no onset; free syllables have no codas, and those made up of a single vowel practically have only the peak. As to the sequences of consonantal elements, a distinction should be made between those which occur as clusters in the onset or the coda of the same syllable and those which occur in transyllabic position, that is, across the coda of a syllable and the onset of the adjoining one.

Besides the single vowel nuclei shown in Figure 2.2, Portuguese has a rich gamut of complex syllable nuclei, formed by a vowel phone accompanied by one or two glides. Phonetically, a glide is produced by a movement of the tongue toward or away from the area of articulation of one of the high vowels [i] or [u]. Such a complex nucleus is a rising diphthong if the glide precedes the vowel, as in quatro ['kwatřu], or a falling diphthong if the glide follows, as in pai [pay]. If two glides are involved, the syllable nucleus is a triphthong, as in the last syllable of Paraguai [pařa'gway].

The phonetic stability of Portuguese diphthongs is a relative matter which depends on varying factors such as style and tempo of speech. By and large, falling diphthongs (Figure 2.5) are more stable than rising ones (Figure 2.6), and stressed diphthongs more than unstressed ones, which can easily be resolved into disyllabic vowel sequences (Câmara 1970: 45-46). Rising diphthongs, as well as triphthongs, are more stable when preceded by a velar consonant than by a consonant of a different point of articulation. This, however, is not a hard and fast rule: the ordinary pronunciation of words like sagüi, quota, and quociente involves diphthongs ([wi], [wɔ], [wo]), but cueca is either [ku-'ɛ-kə] or ['kwɛ-kə], and deságüe becomes [di-za-'gu-i] rather than [di-'za-gwi] in ordinary speech. Likewise, triphthongs are even less stable and can easily be rendered as a disyllabic sequence of diphthong + vowel. Triphthongs beginning with a front glide are least stable, besides being rather rare. Figures 2.6 and 2.7 list examples of such alternations.

Figure 2.5 Falling diphthongs.

/iu/	[iw]	faliu	/ul/	[uw]*	pulga
/ei/	[ey]	sei	/ui/	[uy]	Rui
/eu/	[ew]	seu	/oi/	[oy]	foi
/ɛi/	[ɛy]	réis	/ou/	[ow]**	sou
/ɛu/	[ɛw]	véu	/ɔi/	[ɔy]	dói
/ai/	[ay]	pai	/ɔu/	[ɔw]*	sol
/au/	[aw]	mau			

*The off-glide in the diphthongs [uw] and [ɔw] results from the velarization of syllable-final /l/. See Section 2.6.1.
**In the ordinary language, however, including cultivated speech, the diphthong /ou/ is usually actualized as /o/, e.g. falou [fa'lo], outro ['otřu].

Phonological interpretations of complex syllables have diverged on two issues: (1) whether glides should be considered independent phonemes or allophonic variants of the

Figure 2.6 Rising diphthongs alternating with hiatuses.

	Stressed		Unstressed	
	After velar consonant	After nonvelar consonant		Possible alternation
/ui/	sagüi	juízo	ajuizado	[u-i] ~ [wi]
/ue/	aguento	dueto	duetista	[u-e] ~ [we]
/uɛ/	cueca	sueco		[u-ɛ] ~ [wɛ]
/ua/	enxaguar	suave	suavidade	[u-a] ~ [wa]
/uɔ/	quota			[u-ɔ] ~ [wɔ]
/uo/	quociente	tempestuoso	duodeno	[u-o] ~ [wo]
/iu/		miúdo	miudeza	[i-u] ~ [yu]
/ie/		piegas	piedade	[i-e] ~ [ye]
/iɛ/	quieto	biela		[i-ɛ] ~ [yɛ]
/ia/	quiabo	piaba	piabada	[i-a] ~ [ya]
/iɔ/		idiota		[i-ɔ] ~ [yɔ]
/io/		piolho	piolhento	[i-o] ~ [yo]

Figure 2.7 Triphthongs.

	After velar consonant	After nonvelar consonant	Possible alternation
/uai/	quais	suais	[u-ay] ~ [way]
/uei/	aguei	suei	[u-ey] ~ [wey]
/uou/	aguou	suou	[u-ow] ~ [wow]
/uiu/	arguiu	ruiu	[u-iw] ~ [wiw]
/iai/	guiais	fiais	[i-ay] ~ [yay]
/iei/	guiei	fiei	[i-ey] ~ [yey]
/iou/	guiou	fiou	[i-ow] ~ [yow]

high vowels /i/ and /u/, and (2) whether glides should be included among the vowels or the consonants. Clearly, the second question is relevant only if one chooses to set up the glides as phonemes in the underlying representation. This was the solution originally suggested by Câmara (1953), who considered them vocalic phonemes, although he later reinterpreted them as 'asyllabic ... positional variants of /i/ and /u/' (Câmara 1972:54). Head (1964), on the contrary, made a case for ascribing to /y/ and /w/ the status of phonological consonantal phonemes (while, however, recognizing them as phonetic vowels). This solution would lead to the interpretation of falling diphthongs as sequences of vowel + consonant. Câmara (1970:35-36) considered this solution unsatisfactory, pointing out that whereas it is possible for an '/r/ brando' (that is, a flapped [ř]) to occur after a diphthong in syllable-initial position, only the so-called '/r/ forte'[6] can occur in that position after a consonant (e.g. Israel, guelra).

Other structuralist analyses (Hall 1943, Reed and Leite 1947, Rameh 1962, Feldman 1967, and Hensey 1972) have tended to consider [y] and [w] as asyllabic variants of /i/ and /u/, and a similar interpretation has been shown to hold in a generative framework (Hensey 1968, Vandresen 1974). Mateus (1975) defines those glides as [-syllabic] and [-consonantal], and includes them in the overall phonological inventory.

The case for postulating [y] and [w] as independent phonemes, in one framework or another, depends on a small handful of contrasts which obtain primarily in educated, deliberate speech. A list of those contrasts would include the following items (Câmara 1953:72-75, Head 1964:57ff.).

(2.8a) Verb forms:

vou	[vow]	vs.	vôo	['vou]
sou	[sow]	vs.	sôo	['sou]
dou	[dow]	vs.	dôo	['dou]
sois	[soys]	vs.	soes	['sois]

(2.8b) Verb form vs. verb form + clitic:

deu	[dew]	vs.	dê-o	['deu]
leu	[lew]	vs.	lê-o	['leu]
seu	[sew]	vs.	sê-o	['seu]

(2.8c) Present indicative third person forms of -<u>ar</u> verbs vs. present subjunctive third person forms of -<u>uir</u> verbs:

estatui	[ista'tuy]	vs.	acentue	[asẽ'tui]
possui	[po'suy]	vs.	sue	['sui]
rui	[r̄uy]	vs.	arrue	[a'r̄ui]

Even assuming that there are dialects in which such contrasts are consistently functional, it is possible to account for glides as deriving from one of the underlying vowels /i/ and /u/, as the case may be, when the latter occur unstressed in the same syllable as another vowel. This solution was adumbrated by Head (1964:59), who preferred not to set up a syllable boundary marker in his phonemic analysis. By using such a device, one can say that in the phonological representation of the diphthongs there are two vowels in the same syllable, of which the one specified as [+high] becomes [-syllabic] and surfaces as a glide. The glides [y] and [w] are thus distinguished from [i] and [u] by the feature [-syllabic] (Hensey 1968, Mateus 1975), introduced by a rule such as (2.9), where $ represents a syllabic boundary and the dots (...) indicate that other segments may be present. Since this is a mirror image rule (Sloat et al. 1978:152), it accounts for both rising and falling diphthongs.

(2.9) $$\begin{bmatrix} +\text{syl} \\ +\text{high} \\ \langle \alpha\text{back} \rangle \\ -\text{stress} \end{bmatrix} \rightarrow [-\text{syl}] \ * \ / \ \$ \ (\ldots) \begin{bmatrix} +\text{syl} \\ \left\{ \begin{matrix} -\text{high} \\ \langle +\text{high} \\ -\alpha\text{back} \rangle \end{matrix} \right\} \end{bmatrix} \underline{\qquad} \ (\ldots) \ \$$$

In order to understand how Rule (2.9) accounts for diphthong formation, it should be noticed that while the falling diphthongs of certain words are always stable (e.g. pai, céu), those of others, as well as rising diphthongs in general, alternate between a monosyllabic and a disyllabic (that is, hiatus) pronunciation. Thus, raizame and reunido may be syllabified either as rai-za-me, reu-ni-do or ra-i-za-me, re-u-ni-do, and the sequences of high vowel followed by a nonhigh vowel, as in duetista and piedade, for example, yield both due-tis-ta, pie-da-de and du-e-tis-ta, pi-e-da-de.

The explanation adopted here for such alternation postulates that in the underlying representation contiguous vowels come either with an intervening syllable boundary (V \$ V) or without it (V V). In the latter case one of the vowels is necessarily [+high], and if the other is also [+high], they must contrast as regards the feature [back], as shown by the angle brackets in Rule (2.9). Actually, that rule stands for the combination of several particular rules, whose respective formats and outputs are shown in (2.10).

(2.10a)

$$\underset{/u/}{\begin{bmatrix}+\text{syl}\\+\text{high}\\+\text{back}\end{bmatrix}} \rightarrow \underset{[w]}{[-\text{syl}]} \;/\; \left\{\begin{array}{ll}\underset{/e\ \varepsilon\ a\ \text{ɔ}\ o/}{\begin{bmatrix}+\text{syl}\\-\text{high}\end{bmatrix}}\ \_\_ & \text{yielding: [ew εw aw ɔw ow]}\\ \_\_\ \begin{bmatrix}+\text{syl}\\-\text{high}\end{bmatrix} & \text{yielding: [we wε wa wɔ wo]}\end{array}\right.$$

(2.10b)

$$\underset{/i/}{\begin{bmatrix}+\text{syl}\\+\text{high}\\-\text{back}\end{bmatrix}} \rightarrow \underset{[y]}{[-\text{syl}]} \;/\; \left\{\begin{array}{ll}\underset{/e\ \varepsilon\ a\ \text{ɔ}\ o/}{\begin{bmatrix}+\text{syl}\\-\text{high}\end{bmatrix}}\ \_\_ & \text{yielding: [ey εy ay ɔy oy]}\\ \_\_\ \begin{bmatrix}+\text{syl}\\-\text{high}\end{bmatrix} & \text{yielding: [ye yε ya yɔ yo]}\end{array}\right.$$

(2.10c)

$$\underset{/u/}{\begin{bmatrix}+\text{syl}\\+\text{high}\\+\text{back}\end{bmatrix}} \rightarrow \underset{[w]}{[-\text{syl}]} \;/\; \left\{\begin{array}{ll}\underset{/i/}{\begin{bmatrix}+\text{syl}\\+\text{high}\\-\text{back}\end{bmatrix}}\ \_\_ & \text{yielding: [iw] (e.g. miu-de-za)}\\ \_\_\ \begin{bmatrix}+\text{syl}\\+\text{high}\\-\text{back}\end{bmatrix} & \text{yielding: [wi] (e.g. jui-za-do)}\end{array}\right.$$

(2.10d)

/i/ [y] /u/

$$\begin{bmatrix}+\text{syl}\\+\text{high}\\-\text{back}\end{bmatrix} \rightarrow [-\text{syl}] \;/\; \left\{ \begin{array}{ll} \begin{bmatrix}+\text{syl}\\+\text{high}\\+\text{back}\end{bmatrix}\_\_ & \text{yielding: [uy] (e.g. jui-za-do)} \\ \_\_\begin{bmatrix}+\text{syl}\\+\text{high}\\+\text{back}\end{bmatrix} & \text{yielding: [yu] (e.g. miu-de-za)} \end{array}\right.$$

If the underlying form is of the type $ ... V $ V ... $, the vowel sequence surfaces as a hiatus (as in pi-e-da-de, ra-i-za-me). This solution is obligatory if the two vowels are [-high], since there may not be two such vowels in the same syllable. If one of them is [+high], either the preceding solution applies, yielding a surface hiatus, or the syllable boundary is deleted, and a configuration like $ ... VV ... $ arises which serves as input to Rule (2.9).

2.5 Nasalization. Few topics of Portuguese phonology have received so many different interpretations as the question of nasal vowels. However, it has been shown (Vandresen 1974) that such divergence is due more to differences in the theoretical approach adopted by authors than to differences in the phonetic facts, even though some details of these are not universally agreed upon.[7]

With regard to the phonetics of nasalization (or rather of syllabic nuclei, since nasalized diphthongs are also involved), there are three cases to be considered. First, there are the nasalized nuclei adjacent to a nasal consonant in the following syllable, in words like doma ['dõmə] or boina ['bõỹnə]. The degree of nasalization varies from one individual to another, and the tendency to nasalize the nucleus is greater when the latter is stressed than when it is unstressed (Vandresen 1974: 87-88). The examples in Figure 2.8 show both possibilities.

This type of nasalization results from assimilation of the nucleus to the nasal consonant, and may be summed up by Rule (2.11).

$$\text{(2.11)}\quad [+\text{syl}] \begin{bmatrix}-\text{syl}\\-\text{cns}\end{bmatrix} \rightarrow [+\text{nas}]\ ([+\text{nas}]) \;/\; \_\_\ \$ \begin{bmatrix}+\text{cns}\\+\text{nas}\end{bmatrix}$$

There is some variation among dialects as regards the possibility of stressed nasalized [ɔ] occurring in the environment to the right of the slash in (2.11). In Carioca speech, [o] is the norm (Câmara 1953:77, Head 1964:179f.), whereas for some speakers of Mineiro and Paulista both possibilities exist, although in this case nasalization is less frequent and rather slight. Thus, words like António,[8] estróina may have either oral [ɔ], [ɔy] or slightly nasalized [ɔ̃], [ɔ̃ỹ].

Figure 2.8 Variation in degree of nasalization.

Syllabic nucleus	Stressed	Unstressed
/i/	fino ['fĩnu] ~ ['finu]	final [fi'naw]
/e/	pena ['pẽnə] ~ ['penə]	penado [pe'nadu]
/a/	lama ['lɐ̃mə] ~ ['ləmə]	lamaçal [lama'saw]
/ɔ/	toma ['tɔ̃mə] ~ ['tɔmə]*	tomado [to'madu]
/o/	dona ['dõnə] ~ ['donə]	doninha [do'niñə]
/u/	número ['nũmeṙu] ~ ['numeṙu]	numeral [nume'ṙaw]
/ai/	amaina [amɐ̃ỹnə] ~ [aməynə]	amainado [aməy'nadu]
/ei/	reino ['r̄ẽỹnu] ~ ['r̄eynu]	reinado [r̄ey'nadu]
/oi/	acoima [a'kõỹmə] ~ [akoymə]	acoimado [akoy'madu]
/ui/	arruína [a'r̄ũỹnə] ~ [a'r̄uynə]	arruinado [ar̄uy'nadu]

*There is alternation between [o] and [ɔ] in words like toma, come, fome, etc., according to the dialect. Carioca usually has [o] in such cases, but in Paulista and Mineiro either vowel is possible.

Second, there are nasalized nuclei also in syllable-final position but adjacent to a nonnasal consonant in the following syllable. In such cases, standard orthography represents the nasalized nuclei as vowel + nasal consonant (cf. campo, canto) and, indeed, in slower, paused speech, it is possible to perceive, in the same syllable as the nasal nucleus, a nasal stricture of consonantal nature, homorganic to the following consonant if this is [p b t d k g f v]. That stricture can be transcribed phonetically as a superscript, as in campo ['kɐ̃^{m}pu], canto ['kɐ̃^{n}tu], cancro [kɐ̃^{ŋ}kṙu]. In fast speech, however, that stricture tends to become blurred and to disappear altogether. If the consonant following the phonological nasal vowel is other than those listed, the phonetic nasal stricture is practically nonexistent in the dialects considered here.[9]

The presence of a nasal consonantal stricture has been pointed out by several authors, among them Nobiling (1903), Reed and Leite (1943), Wise (1957), Câmara (1953, 1969, 1970, 1972), and Vandresen (1974). Implicitly or explicitly, these authors agree that this consonantal element is syllable-final; only Hall (1943) interprets it as a prenasalization feature of the following occlusive.

In the position under consideration there is no functional contrast among the nasal consonant-like strictures, regardless of how prominent they may be, since their articulation is always homorganic with the following consonant. This lack of contrast has made it possible for some authors to postulate for that position either an archiphoneme (Câmara 1953, 1969, 1970, 1972; Barbosa 1962), or, within the generative framework, a segment specified only as [+cns, +nas] (Mateus 1975,[10] Hensey 1968).

The present analysis postulates a fully specified consonant segment following the vocalic nucleus, and makes nasalization a consequence of a rule such as (2.12a). Since the only two available nasals, /n/ and /m/, do not contrast in this environment, it is immaterial which of them is chosen for the underlying representation. Any nasal in this position is subject to a rule like (2.12b), where P.A. is an ad hoc symbol meaning the same point in the articulation.

(2.12a) $[+\text{syl}] \rightarrow [+\text{nas}] \; / \; \_\_ \begin{bmatrix} +\text{cns} \\ +\text{nas} \end{bmatrix} \$ \; ([+\text{cns}])$

(2.12b) $\begin{bmatrix} +\text{cns} \\ +\text{nas} \end{bmatrix} \rightarrow [\text{P.A.}] \; / \; \_\_ \; \$ \begin{bmatrix} +\text{cns} \\ \text{P.A.} \end{bmatrix}$

Rule (2.12b) makes the nasal consonant homorganic with the following consonant. Once this rule has applied, one will have /m/ before the bilabial obstruents /p/ and /b/, and /n/ in all other cases. Consequently, no harm is done if, as a matter of visual convenience, one chooses to transcribe that nasal consonant as /m/ in words like *campa* /kampa/ or *samba* /samba/ and as /n/ elsewhere, as in *canta* /kanta/ or *canga* /kanga/. The realization of the nasal consonant as a consonantal stricture is the function of a rule like (2.13), which applies after (2.12b).

(2.13) $\begin{bmatrix} +\text{cns} \\ +\text{nas} \\ \text{P.A.} \end{bmatrix} \rightarrow \begin{bmatrix} +\text{cns} \\ +\text{nas} \\ +\text{reduced} \end{bmatrix} \; / \; \_\_ \; \$ \begin{bmatrix} +\text{cns} \\ \text{P.A.} \end{bmatrix}$

Thus, the generation of words like *campa*, *canta*, and *canga* would include the operations shown in (2.14).

(2.14)	*campa*	*canta*	*canga*	
	/kanpa/	/kanta/	/kanga/	underlying form
	kampa	kanta	kaŋga	assimilation of nasal consonant to the following consonant
	'kãmpa	'kãnta	'kãŋga	nasalization
	'kə̃mpa	'kə̃nta	'kə̃ŋga	raising of nasalized /a/ → [ə]
	'kə̃mpə	'kə̃ntə	'kə̃ŋgə	raising of final unstressed /a/ → [ə]
	['kə̃ᵐpə]	['kə̃ⁿtə]	['kə̃ᵑge]	reduction of the nasal consonant to a stricture
	['kə̃pə]	['kə̃tə]	['kə̃gə]	deletion of nasal stricture

It should be noticed that this analysis accounts for a common feature of colloquial and/or rural speech, namely, the emergence of a surface nasal consonant, [m] or [n] as the case may be, after the loss of an occlusive segment in syllable-initial position, as in the words shown in (2.15a).[11]

(2.15a) +*tamém* [tə'mẽỹ] < *também*
+*istamo* [is'tə̃mu] < +*istambo* < *estômago*
+*quanu* ['kwə̃nu] < *quando*
+*cuminação* [kũmina'sə̃w̃] < *combinação*

Another similar common phenomenon is the reduction of the present participle desinence *Vndo* to *Vno* in forms such as (2.15b), which reflects a productive process far more widespread, even among educated speakers, than is usually acknowledged.[12]

(2.15b) *falando* /falando/ → +*falano* [fa'lə̃nu]
correndo /kor̃endo/ → +*correno* [ko'r̃ẽnu]
partindo /partindo/ → +*partino* [par'tĩnu]

The third and final case, that of nasalized syllable nuclei in word-final position, is interpreted like the second, that is, as a sequence of a simple or complex nucleus followed by an underlying /n/.

Figure 2.9 Nasalized syllable nuclei in word-final position.

Key word	Phonological representation of nucleus	Phonetic realization of nucleus
fim	/fin/	[fĩ(ñ)] ~ [fĩỹ(ñ)]
tem	/en/	[ẽỹ(ñ)]
tenda		[ẽ^{n}]
mãe	/ain/	[ə̃ỹ(ñ)]
lã	/an/	[ə̃(ŋ)]
mão	/aun/	[ə̃w̃(ŋ)]
som	/on/	[õw̃(ŋ)]
		[õ(ŋ)]
põe	/oin/	[õỹ(ñ)]
dum	/un/	[ũ(ŋ)]
		[ũw̃(ŋ)]
ruim*	/uin/	[ũỹ(ñ)]

*There are very few words with this diphthong. One is *muito* [mũỹ^{n}tu], the result of progressive assimilation of the initial nasal consonant. Another is *ruim*, which also has a (normative) standard pronunciation with hiatus, [r̃u'ĩ^{ñ}]. Both have a few derivatives, e.g. *ruindade*, *ruinzeira*, *muitissimo*. *Mui* [mũỹ^{ñ}] is exclusively a literary item.

As shown in Figure 2.9, the phonetic realizations of these nuclei fall into three categories. First there are those which correspond consistently to phonetic diphthongs, and for which the sequences /ain/, /aun/, /oin/, and /uin/ are postulated. To the second set belong the sequences /in/, /un/, and /an/, which are always manifested as single nasalized vowels (although under stress the first two may be lengthened or slightly diphthongized). The last set includes two items, /on/ and /en/, either of which can surface as a single vowel or a diphthong. A nasal consonant stricture may be present in all cases, and it is either a palatal [ñ] after a front vowel or a velar [ŋ] after a nonfront vowel. Given this distribution, the phonetic shape of the nasal which originates that stricture can be explained by a rule such as (2.16).

(2.16) $$\begin{bmatrix}[\text{-syl}]\\ \\ [\text{+nas}]\end{bmatrix} \rightarrow \left\{\begin{array}{l}[\tilde{n}]\ /\ \begin{bmatrix}\text{+syl}\\ \text{+front}\end{bmatrix}\ \_\_\ \#\\ \\ [n]\ /\ \begin{bmatrix}\text{+syl}\\ \text{-front}\end{bmatrix}\ \_\_\ \#\end{array}\right.$$

The postulation of both the nasal consonant and the stricture it originates is justified by the fact that, whereas the latter is normally dropped in absolute word-final position, it is quite noticeable as less than a full-fledged nasal consonant preceding a vowel in a following word, in sequences such as those in (2.17).

(2.17) fim horrível [fĩ^{n}o'r̃ivew ~ [fĩo'r̃ivew]
tem isso [tẽỹ^{ñ}'isu] ~ [tẽỹ'isu]
ruim assim [r̃ũỹ^{ñ}a'sĩ] ~ [r̃ũỹa'sĩ]
nem um[13] [nẽỹñ'ũ] ~ [nẽỹ'ũ]
nem uma[13] [nẽỹñ'ũmə] ~ [nẽỹ'ũmə]

The set of rules involving the underlying /n/ can be summarized as follows. As in Rule (2.12a), it nasalizes the preceding syllable nucleus and then it originates a specific nasal consonant, as in Rule (2.16). Next, a reduction rule changes this consonant into a brief consonant stricture (2.18) which is optional if a vowel follows and is obligatorily deleted at utterance-final position.[14]

(2.18) $$\left\{\begin{array}{l}[\tilde{n}]\\ [\text{ŋ}]\end{array}\right\} \rightarrow \left\{\begin{array}{l}[\tilde{n}]\\ [\text{ŋ}]\end{array}\right\}\ /\ \_\_\ \#$$

Only four complex nuclei, /ai/, /au/, /oi/, and /ui/, are needed in the underlying representation (Almeida 1976:378f.), and their phonetic realization follows the same sequence of rules, that is, diphthongization (Rule 2.9) and nasalization (Rule 2.12a). The phonetic form of nasalized /ai/ is [ãỹ], as a result of a reduction rule whose representation would be as in (2.19).

(2.19)
$$\begin{bmatrix}\text{+syl}\\ \text{+low}\\ \text{-front}\\ \text{-back}\end{bmatrix} \rightarrow [\text{-low}] \;/\; \underline{\quad}\; (\$) \begin{bmatrix}\text{+cns}\\ \text{+nas}\end{bmatrix}$$

Likewise, /i u a/ + nasal require only the nasalization Rule (2.12a), followed by automatic application of the reduction Rule (2.2) in the case of /an/, before the rules concerning /n/ apply.

A slight complication involves nasal nuclei formed by a vowel specified as [-low], [-high]. The sequence /en/ in final position corresponds phonetically to [ey(ñ)] when stressed, as in armazém, and to either [ey(ñ)] or [ĩ(ñ)] when unstressed, as in sem (e.g. sem amigos [s̃ẽy(ñ)a'migus], [sĩ(ñ)a'migus]). Furthermore, in nonfinal position, stressed or not, as in tenda or tendinha, the underlying /e/ + nasal may surface as [ẽỹ(n)] or [ẽ(n)].[15]

The appearance of the phonetic glide can be described by Rule (2.20), which inserts /i/ between /e/ and the nasal in the underlying representation.

(2.20)
$$\emptyset \rightarrow \begin{bmatrix}\text{+syl}\\ \text{+high}\\ \text{+front}\end{bmatrix} \;/\; \begin{bmatrix}\text{+syl}\\ \text{-high}\\ \text{-low}\\ \text{+front}\\ \alpha\text{stress}\end{bmatrix} \underline{\quad} \begin{bmatrix}\text{+cns}\\ \text{+nas}\end{bmatrix} \begin{Bmatrix}\#\\ \$\end{Bmatrix}$$

Condition: Rule (2.20) is obligatory if # and $\alpha = +$ obtain, and optional otherwise.

Likewise, the nucleus derived from /on/ may be either a diphthong [õw̃] or a single vowel [õ], with the difference that this alternation is optional regardless of stress, e.g. tom [tõw̃(n)] ~ [to(n)], tonto ['tõw̃(n)tu] ~ ['tõ(n)tu], tontice [tõw̃(n)tɪsi] ~ [tõ(n)'tisi].[16] Rule (2.21) would apply in this case.

(2.21)
$$\emptyset \rightarrow \begin{bmatrix}\text{+syl}\\ \text{+high}\\ \text{-front}\end{bmatrix} \;/\; \begin{bmatrix}\text{+syl}\\ \text{-high}\\ \text{-low}\\ \text{-front}\end{bmatrix} \underline{\quad} \begin{bmatrix}\text{+cns}\\ \text{+nas}\end{bmatrix}$$

The derivation of the different nasalized nuclei seen in this section may be summarized as in Figure 2.10.

2.6 Consonants. The Portuguese consonant system has been variously described as including from 16 to 21 distinctive units. That variation is due to competing interpretations of the phonological status of [l̃], [ñ], [r̄] (the so-called 'double' or 'strong' r of words like roupa, carro, and honra) and the glides [y] and [w]. This study adopts the figure of 19

Figure 2.10 Derivation of nasalized nuclei.

Underlying representation	Insertion of /i,u/	Diphthong-ization	Nasali-zation	Reduction of nasalized [a] → [ə]	Formation of nasal consonant	Reduction of nasal consonant to a stricture	Deletion of nasal stricture
/ain/	–	ayn	ãỹn	ə̃ỹn	ə̃ỹñ	[ə̃ỹ^{ñ}]	[ə̃ỹ]
/aun/	–	awn	ãw̃n	ə̃w̃n	ə̃w̃ŋ	[ə̃w̃^{ŋ}]	[ə̃w̃]
/oin/	–	oyn	õỹn	–	õỹñ	[õỹ^{ñ}]	[õỹ]
/uin/	–	uyn	ũỹn	–	ũỹñ	[ũỹ^{ñ}]	[ũỹ]
/en/	ei	eyn	ẽyn	–	ẽỹñ	[ẽỹ^{ñ}]	[ẽỹ]
	–	–	ẽn	–		[ẽ^{n}]	[ẽ]
/on/	ou	own	õw̃n	–	õw̃ŋ	[õw̃^{ŋ}]	[õw̃]
	–	–	õn	–		[õ^{ŋ}]	[õ]
/in/	–	–	ĩn	–	ĩñ	[ĩ^{ñ}]	[ĩ]
/un/	–	–	ũn	–	ũŋ	[ũ^{ŋ}]	[ũ]
/an/	–	–	ãn	ə̃n	ə̃ŋ	[ə̃^{ŋ}]	[ə̃]

consonant phonemes, with /l̃/, /ñ/, and /r̄/ considered as independent phonological units, and the glides, as was seen in Section 2.4, as positional variants of the high vowels /i/ and /u/.

The description of consonants takes into account two broad parameters, namely, manner and position (or area) of articulation. The following contrasts in manner, each of which corresponds to a distinctive feature, are relevant here.

(a) Continuant vs. occlusive. Continuant sounds are articulated without interrupting the flow of egressive lung air as it goes through the oral cavity. If the articulators form an obstacle capable of preventing the air from passing through, the consonant is an occlusive or [-continuant], such as [p t k b d g].

(b) Nasal vs. oral. Nasal consonants are articulated with the velum lowered, so that the air enters the nasal cavity through the nasopharynx. Otherwise, if the velum is raised, the sound is oral or [-nasal]. Since Portuguese nasal consonants are articulated with occlusion of the oral cavity, they may be considered a subclass of [-continuant] consonants.

(c) Sonorant. This feature refers to the possibility of spontaneous voicing taking place during the articulation of a sound, and it is shared by vowels, glides, and certain consonants like [l] and [l̃].

(d) Lateral. In the articulation of lateral sounds, the air flows around the sides of the obstruction in the oral cavity, as in [l] and [l̃].

(e) Vibrant. This feature refers to sounds produced by vibration of the tongue. In Portuguese it applies to only two sounds, namely, the flapped r of cara ['kaɾə] and the 'double' r of carro, which in one of its phonetic manifestations is an alveolar trill [r̄].

(f) Voicing. Depending on whether or not the vocal cords vibrate, sounds are classified as [+voiced] or [-voiced].

Regarding the position of articulation, six categories are relevant, namely:

(a) Bilabial: The articulators are the lips, which act together to block the airflow, as in [b], [p], and [m].

(b) Labiodental: the lower front teeth form an obstacle with the upper lip, as in [v], and [f].

(c) Apicodental: the apex of the tongue touches the inner face of the front teeth, as in [t] and [d].

(d) Laminoalveolar: the blade of the tongue is placed against the alveolar ridge, as in [l], [n], [s], [z].

(e) Palatal: the pre-dorsum of the tongue touches the hard palate, as in [l̃].

(f) Dorsovelar: the post-dorsum of the tongue touches the velum, as in [k] and [g].

The combination of these positions and manners of articulation yields the articulatory classification of consonants shown in Figure 2.11. That figures includes two additional manners of articulation, glottal and uvular, and three more symbols, [h], [x], and [R], which stand for variants of [r̄]. (See Section 2.6.1, under /r̄/.) It also includes, for ease of reference, the traditional names for nonnasal noncontinuants (stops) and nonsonorant continuants (fricatives).

The articulatory classification shown in Figure 2.11, while very practical for many purposes, is somewhat redundant. For example, stops and nasals can be grouped together as [-continuant]. Furthermore, position of articulation can be classified in terms of two features only, namely, [anterior] and [coronal]. Anterior sounds are articulated in front of the palatoalveolar region, like [p b t d n l ṙ r̄ s z]. Coronal sounds are articulated with the tip of the blade raised from its rest position, as in [t d n ñ r r̄ š ž]. By using a binary distinctive feature approach, one arrives at a complete classification of Portuguese consonants involving only nonredundant features, as shown in Figure 2.12. These features can be organized in matrices, each of which defines a specific consonant. All Portuguese consonants are by definition [+cons] and [-syl]. The latter feature indicates that a Portuguese consonant cannot constitute the nucleus of a syllable. Figure 2.13 shows the distinctive feature matrices of Portuguese consonant phonemes.

2.6.1 Phonetic realization of consonants. Like the vowels, the consonant phonemes are affected, in varying degrees, by the phonological environment in which they occur. In this section, I analyze the more important variants of their phonetic realizations.

/p/: a voiceless bilabial nonnasal obstruent [p], as in para ['paṙə], capa ['kapə].

/b/: a voiced bilabial nonnasal obstruent [b], as in boi [boy], aba ['abə].

/t/: a voiceless apicodental nonnasal obstruent [t], as in tala ['talə], até [a'tɛ]. Before the high front vowel [i], this is the conservative realization of this phoneme, as in tio ['tiu]; however, in most of the area considered, it undergoes several degrees of palatalization. In Paulista and Mineiro, palatalization varies, when it occurs, from a slightly affricated [t^{š}] articulated in the prepalatal region to a full affricate, [č], which is its normal realization in Carioca, as in tia ['čiə].

/d/: a voiced apicodental obstruent [d], as in [dado] ['dadu]. Like its voiceless counterpart, and in the same areas already mentioned, it palatalizes before [i] as in dia ['d^{ǰ}iə], ['ǰiə]. In such cases, palatalization may be described as resulting from a change in the value of the feature [anterior], according to Rule (2.22).

(2.22)
$$\begin{bmatrix} +\text{cons} \\ -\text{cont} \\ +\text{ant} \\ +\text{cor} \end{bmatrix} \rightarrow [-\text{ant}] \;/\; \underline{\quad} \begin{bmatrix} +\text{syl} \\ +\text{high} \\ +\text{front} \end{bmatrix}$$

Figure 2.11 Articulatory classification of Portuguese consonants.

			position: / manner	bilabial		labiodental		apicodental		laminoalveolar		palatal		dorsovelar		glottal	uvular
				vl	vd	vl	vd	vl	vd	vl	vd	vl	vd	vl	vd		
consonant	noncontinuant	nonsonorant	stops	p	b			t	d					k	g		
consonant	noncontinuant	sonorant	nasals		m				n				ñ				
consonant	continuant	nonsonorant	fricatives			f	v			s	z	š	ž	(x)		(h)	
consonant	continuant	sonorant	lateral						l				l̃				
consonant	continuant	sonorant	flap						ṙ								
consonant	continuant	sonorant	trill						r̄								(R)

Figure 2.12 Distinctive features of Portuguese consonants.

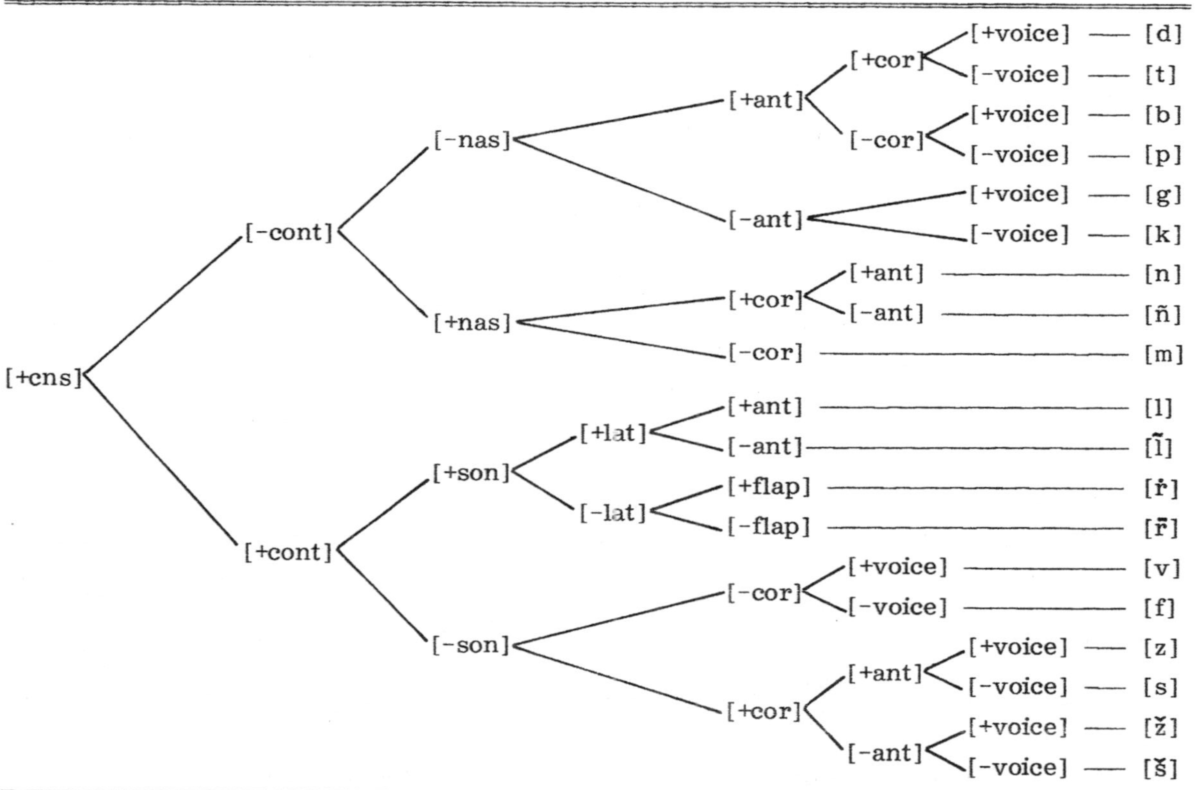

Figure 2.13 Distinctive feature specifications of Portuguese consonants.

	p	b	t	d	k	g	m	n	ñ	f	v	s	z	š	ž	l	l̃	ṙ	r̄	(x)	(R)	(h)
consonantal	+	+	+	+	+	+	+	+	+	+	+	+	+	+	+	+	+	+	+	+	+	+
syllabic	−	−	−	−	−	−	−	−	−	−	−	−	−	−	−	−	−	−	−	−	−	−
sonorant	−	−	−	−	−	−	+	+	+	−	−	−	−	−	−	+	+	+	−			
continuant	−	−	−	−	−	−	−	−	−	+	+	+	+	+	+	+	+	+	+	+	+	+
anterior	+	+	+	+	−	−	+	+	−	+	+	+	+	−	−	+	−	+	+	−	−	−
coronal	−	−	+	+	−	−	−	+	+	−	−	+	+	+	+	+	+	+	+	−	−	−
nasal	−	−	−	−	−	−	+	+	+	−	−	−	−	−	−	−	−	−	−	−	−	−
lateral																+	+					
flap																		+	−			
voiced	−	+	−	+	−	+	+	+	+	−	+	−	+	−	+	+	+	+	+	−	−	−

/k/: a voiceless dorsovelar obstruent, [k], as in *cada* ['kadə], or prevelar, [k˂], by assimilation to a following [i], as in *aqui* [a'k˂i].

/g/: a voiced dorsovelar obstruent, [g], as in *gado* ['gadu], or prevelar, [g˂], by assimilation to a following [i], as in *guia* ['giə].

/f/: a voiceless labiodental continuant, [f], as in *faca* ['fakə].

/v/: a voiceless labiodental continuant, [v], as in *vaca* ['vakə].

/s/: a voiceless laminoalveolar continuant, [s], in syllable-initial position throughout the area considered. In Mineiro and Paulista, it becomes voiced in syllable-final position before a voiced consonant or vowel, as in *às duas* [az'duəs], *às armas* [a'zarməs], and it remains voiceless if followed by a voiceless consonant or pause, as in *este* ['esti], *duas* ['duəs]. The voicing rule can be described as in (2.23).

$$(2.23)\quad \begin{bmatrix} +\text{cns} \\ -\text{son} \\ +\text{cont} \\ +\text{ant} \\ +\text{cor} \\ -\text{voiced} \end{bmatrix} \rightarrow [+\text{voiced}] \;/\; \_\_\_ \;\$\; [+\text{voiced}]$$

In Carioca, the normal realization of /s/ in syllable-final and prepausal position is a voiceless palatal fricative, [š], as in *esta* ['ɛštə], *todos* ['toduš]. This palatalization can be described by a rule like (2.24).

$$(2.24)\quad \begin{bmatrix} +\text{cns} \\ -\text{son} \\ +\text{ant} \end{bmatrix} \rightarrow [-\text{ant}] \;/\; \_\_\_ \begin{Bmatrix} \$ \\ \# \end{Bmatrix}$$

The voicing Rule (2.23) applies regularly in syllable-final position, generating a voiced palatal fricative [ž], as in *desde* ['deǯi], as well as in word-final position, if the next word begins with a voiced consonant: *os dois* [už'doyš]. If it begins with a vowel, however, the palatalization Rule (2.22) does not apply: *os homens* [u'zɔmẽỹš]. If the following word begins with [s] or [z], the palatalization rule may apply, yielding the sequences [š-s] or [ž-z], as in *os sapos* [uš'sapus] and *os zagueiros* [uzža'geyɾus]. If the palatalization rule does not apply, the sequence of identical consonants /s-s/ or /z-z/ yields a single phonetic consonant: *os sapos* [u'sapus], *os zagueiros* [uza'geyɾus].

/z/: a voiced laminoalveolar continuant, [z], as in *zona* ['zonə], *casa* ['kazə].

/š/: a voiceless palatal continuant (fricative), [š], as in *chato* ['šatu], *achado* [a'šadu].

/ž/: a voiced palatal continuant (fricative), [ž], as in jato ['žatu], laje ['laži].

/l/: in prevocalic position, a laminodental voiced lateral, [l], as in lado ['ladu] and ali [a'li]. In postvocalic position, it becomes velarized, with the dorsum of the tongue retracted toward the velum and the underside of the blade resting on the lower alveolar ridge. In very deliberate pronunciation this articulation may yield the velar lateral [ɫ], but in ordinary speech, there is also significant rounding of the lips and the tongue moves toward the velum, articulating a postvocalic back glide [w]. As a result of this, for the majority of speakers there is no difference in pronunciation between mau and mal [maw], or pau and pal(mito) [paw], and so on.

/l̃/: a voiced laminopalatal lateral, [l̃], as in calha ['kal̃ə]. In very casual pronunciation the articulation may be shifted to the alveolar region, forming an [l]-like sound followed by a front glide: malha ['mal^{y}ə]. In nonstandard accents there is a good deal of wavering between [l̃], [l^y] and even [y], with the result that words like malha and Amalia may rhyme, that is, either [a'mal̃ə]:[mal̃ə] or [a'mal^{y}ə]:['malyə] or [a'mayə]:['ma^{y}ə].

/m/: a voiced bilabial nasal obstruent, [m], as in meu [mew], cama ['kə̃mə]. (Concerning postvocalic position, see Section 2.5, Nasalization.)

/n/: a voiced apicodental nasal obstruent, [n], as in cana ['kə̃nə]. (Concerning postvocalic position, see Section 2.5, Nasalization.)

/ñ/: a voiced palatal nasal obstruent, [ñ], as in ganha ['gəñə]. In nonstandard accents, a relaxation in articulation moves the tongue away from the hard palate and toward the alveolar ridge, creating an [n]-like sound followed by a brief glide between that consonant and the following vowel, as in lenha ['len^{y}ə].

/ṙ/: a voiced apicoalveolar flap, [ṙ], as in caro ['kaṙu]. In final position, it is maintained only in educated speech and slow, deliberate styles; otherwise it is greatly reduced, devoiced, or dropped altogether, as in falar [fa'la^ṙ], fa'laṙ̥], [fa'la]. If followed by a word beginning with a vowel, final /r/, if pronounced, links with that vowel, forming a new syllable: falar alguma coisa [fa'laṙaw'gumə'koyzə]. Some speakers have /r̄/ or /x/ in final absolute position: /a'mor̄/, /a'mox/.

In Caipira, /ṙ/ has a palatal retroflexed realization, [ṛ], very similar to that of English /r/: carpa ['kaṛpə]. There is also loss of contrast between /l/ and /r/ in postvocalic position, with replacement of /l/ by /ṙ/, with the result that alma = arma ['aṛmə].

/r̄/: this symbol, which corresponds to an alveolar trill, has been used so far to represent the so-called 'double' r. In fact, this phoneme has several different phonetic renderings, namely:

(1) [r̄]: voiced apicoalveolar trill
[ṝ]: voiceless apicoalveolar trill
(2) [ʁ̇]: voiced alveopalatal fricative, slightly retroflexed
[ʁ̣]: voiceless alveopalatal fricative, slightly retroflexed
(3) [x]: voiceless velar fricative
(4) [R̥]: voiceless uvular trill
(5) [h]: voiceless glottal fricative

All of these sounds are regionally distributed variants of the same phoneme, although with a noticeable amount of overlapping, so that some are found in free variation in the same dialect or even in the speech of the same individual.

The sounds in set (1), [r̄] and [ṝ], correspond to the conservative pronunciation of /r̄/, which alternates with the sounds of the second set in both Paulista and Mineiro. In both these dialects, however, variants (3) and, to a lesser extent, (4) are also found, particularly in the cities of Belo Horizonte and São Paulo, where many speakers use them interchangeably. On the other hand, [x], [R], and [h] are interchangeable in Carioca, where the sounds of (1) and (2) are rare in ordinary speech.

The distinctive contrast between /r/ and /r̄/[17] is maintained only in intervocalic position, as in caro vs. carro. Elsewhere, /r̄/ occurs in absolute initial position and after a consonant (Roberto, honra, Israel, guelra). In other positions, the contrast is neutralized and either phoneme can be realized as any of the variants of either /ṙ/ or /r̄/, as in morto ['mortu], ['mor̄tu], ['moxtu], ['moṙtu], etc., and there is a tendency for some realizations of /r̄/ to predominate in syllable-final position.

2.7 Syllable types. The simplest syllable type in Portuguese contains only one vowel (ex.: há, a-la). If the nucleus is a diphthong, one of the vowels must be, as seen in Section 2.4, both [+high] and [-stressed], and articulated as a phonetic glide. However, Portuguese diphthongs are very unstable (Câmara 1970: 45), and the possibility exists that they be articulated as a sequence of two vowels in adjacent syllables, that is, a hiatus. This is particularly true of rising diphthongs, hence the alternate pronunciation of words such as pátria or suave as either dissyllabic (pá-tria, sua-ve) or trisyllabic (pá-tri-a, su-a-ve). Triphthongs show some stability at word-final position before a pause or a word beginning in a consonant (ex.: Pa-ra-guai-tris-te), but before a vowel they expand easily into a sequence of two rising diphthongs, as in paraguaio ([pa-ra-'gwa-yo]). In very emphatic pronunciation, a sequence of three vowels is possible instead of a triphthong (e.g. U-ru-gu-a-i), but this is an extreme case, and as regards the overall pattern of the language, a marginal phenomenon at best.

As to the sequences of consonantal elements, a distinction should be made between those which occur as clusters in the onset or the coda of the same syllable, and those which occur in transsyllabic position, that is, across the coda of a syllable and the onset of the adjoining one.

If the syllable nucleus is represented by V, and different consonants as C, the syllable types of Portuguese are as in (2.25).

(2.25)	V	há
	VC	as
	CV	dá
	CVC	dás
	CCV	pra (<para)
	CCVC	cruz
	CCVCC	trans- (phonologically /trans-/, phonetically [trə̃$^{(n)}$s])

Not all consonants occur in every position, and the restrictions of occurrence are best understood if single consonants and clusters are considered separately. Single consonants are treated here and clusters are studied in Chapter Five, where they are compared with English clusters. All consonants can come in the onset of a noninitial syllable, and all but /ṙ/ if the syllable is word-initial. In the coda, only /r l s n/ are possible. These possibilities are exemplified in Figure 2.14.[18]

Likewise, the representation of postvocalic nasal consonants can be effected by using only /n/, or /n/ and /m/, or by a nasal archiphoneme /N/ (Câmara 1953), or by an underlying segment specified only for [+cons] and [+nas] (Mateus 1976).

If only /n/ is used, a rule is needed to change it into every one of the nasal consonants which can appear between a nasalized vowel and another consonant. If both /n/ and /m/ are adopted, there would be need for a similar rule which would change /n/ into the other phonetic nasal consonants, with the exception of [m], which would derive from underlying /m/. This solution would entail a slightly more complex underlying representation, as well as the introduction of one more phoneme in the rule for syllables of the (CC)VC- type, but no extra phoneme in the overall inventory, since both /n/ and /m/ are independently motivated anyway. The last two solutions are equivalent, Câmara's archiphoneme and Mateus's incompletely specified segment having, each in its own framework, the same theoretical import. Either solution highlights the neutralization of the contrast [m]:[n] in preconsonantal position, and either rule amounts to the introduction of an extra segment in the overall inventory of phonemes, irrespective of whether these be systematic or autonomous.

NOTES

1. In such cases, /ɛ, ɔ/, while definitely less stressed than the vowel bearing main stress, may retain a stronger degree

Figure 2.14 Occurrence of Portuguese consonants in several positions.

	Absolute initial	Medial	Syllable-final	Absolute final
/p/	pato	capa		
/b/	bata	cabo		
/t/	toca	mato		
/d/	data	cada		
/k/	cata	laca		
/g/	gato	toga		
/m/	mato	cama		
/n/	nata	cana	canto	sã, são (phonol. /san/, /saon/)
/ñ/	nhonhô	minha		
/f/	faca	alfa		
/v/	vaca	alva		
/s/	saga	aço	deste	más
/z/	zaga	vezo	desde	
/š/	chaga	acho		
/ž/	jato	haja		
/l/	lado	mala	alto	sal
/l̃/	lhama	relho		
/ṙ/	...	caro	farto	ser
/r̄/	rato	carro		

of stress than the other syllables in formal speech. This phenomenon, sometimes called secondary stress, is phonologically nondistinctive. See Section 6.2.

2. *Caipira* is the general name of a group of rural dialects spoken in large areas of the states of São Paulo and Minas Gerais. For a characterization, see Amaral (1920), Istre (1971), and Rodrigues (1974).

3. Amaral's spelling has been preserved.

4. Rodrigues's diacritics: [Ṿ], closed vowel; [V̤], very closed vowel; [r̤], retroflexed or cacuminal vibrant liquid.

5. Reduction of /o/ to phonetic [u] in words like *tomate* [tu'mati], *botão* [bu'tə̃w], *jogar* [žu'ga], and so on, seems more common in Mineiro than in Carioca or Paulista.

6. Câmara's argument holds whether the 'strong /r/' is actualized phonetically either as an alveolar trill or as a velar trill or fricative.

7. The dialects represented in the best-known studies are those of Vitória, Espírito Santo (Hall 1943), São Paulo (Reed and Leite 1947, Cintra 1962), Juiz de Fora, Minas Gerais (Rameh 1962), and Rio de Janeiro (Câmara 1953, Head 1964, Wise 1957; the last author makes references to Paulista, which is also taken into account by Feldman 1967). Cumulative reviews of the bibliography on vowel nasalization can be found

in Head (1964), Back (1973), Vandresen (1974), and Almeida (1976). See also Istre (1975).

8. *Antônio*, with stressed [o], is also common.

9. This was noted by Wise (1957:521). In Continental Portuguese, a nasal consonantal stricture has been experimentally identified before all consonants that can occur in a nasalized nucleus followed by a nonnasal consonant (Almeida 1976:365ff.).

10. Mateus (1975:90, n. 50) explains her choice of the symbol /N/ as 'puramente convencional', and that there are reasons to consider that sound a '/n/ (consoante nasal [+cor]).'

11. Nonstandard (colloquial and/or rural) forms are indicated by a raised (⁺). Both ⁺*estamo* and ⁺*estambo* occur in rural speech. Though they are diachronically derived from standard *estômago*, it is reasonable to postulate that speakers who do not have the latter in their lexicon have instead a lexical entry like /estambo/.

12. 'In colloquial style, both in urban and in rural areas of Brazil, particularly the Northeast, the present participle ending is reduced to [-nu]' (Gomes de Matos 1970:441).

13. As opposed to the lexicalized forms *nenhum* and *nenhuma*, whose diachronic origin, however, is to be explained by the full articulation of palatal [ñ] (Câmara 1972:57).

14. This is somewhat of a simplification. In all likelihood, (2.18) functions as a variable rule in either environment. The circumstances determining such variation are probably rather complex and depend on factors such as speech tempo, style, register, emphasis, and so on.

15. Vandresen (1974:89). The [y] glide, if present at all, is in this case very brief and far less noticeable than in final position. A better transcription would probably be $[\tilde{e}^{(\tilde{y}n)}]$.

16. Stressed /on/ occurs finally in a few monosyllables: *bom*, *dom*, *com*, *tom*, *som*. Elsewhere, the tendency to diphthongize is rather slight, and the phonetic glide is usually a reduced version of [w].

17. Throughout this study the symbol /r̄/ will be used to indicate the phoneme in question, regardless of its specific phonetic characteristics.

18. The inventory of syllable-final consonants would be enlarged if we included /z/ for medial syllables (Mascherpe 1970, Cintra 1978). However, in this position the contrast /z/ vs. /s/ is conditioned by the value of the following consonant as regards voicing, as in *desde* ['dezdi] vs. *deste* ['desti]. In absolute final position, only /s/ appears, but it is voiced by assimilation to a following voiced sound, as in *os dois homens* [uzdoy'zɔmẽỹs]. This variation provided Câmara (1970:42) with the necessary justification for postulating a fricative archiphone /S/ in syllable-final position. In a generative approach, items like *desde* and *este* may be represented with an underlying /s/, which becomes voiced by assimilation.

3

THE SOUNDS OF ENGLISH

3.1 **Introduction.** This chapter presents a brief analysis, in articulatory and distinctive feature terms, of the phonemes of English and their phonetic manifestations. The analysis is limited to aspects of interest for the comparison with Portuguese phonemes presented in Chapter 4. The considerations made earlier about phonological description (Section 1.2) and the classification of Portuguese sounds (Sections 2.2 and 2.6) apply, mutatis mutandis, to the classification of English sounds, and thus need not be repeated here.

3.2 **Syllabic nuclei.** The ensuing presentation follows the precedent of other authors (particularly Agard and Di Pietro 1965, Stockwell and Bowen 1965, and Kufner 1971) in taking as a point of reference a normalized vowel system intended to embody a set of features shared by a majority of speakers of General American English.

A preliminary classification of vocalic syllabic nuclei in stressed position, according to the parameters of tongue height ([high] vs. [low]) and horizontal displacement ([front] vs. [back]), as well as lip rounding ([rounded] vs. [unrounded]), is shown in Figure 3.1. As the phonetic symbols suggest, there are two phonetic types of syllable nuclei, namely, seven simple ones, represented by the single vowels [ɩ ɛ æ a ɔ ω ʌ], and seven complex ones, represented by a vowel followed by either a front glide [y] or a back glide [w]: [iy ey ay aw ɔy ow uw].

Figure 3.1 leaves out a few important characteristics of the nuclei. For example, the vowels represented as [a] and [ʌ] are phonetically more [back] than central. There are also differences between the complex nuclei as regards the realization of the offglides. In [ay] the front upglide, while moving toward the target position of a cardinal [i], usually reaches only a midfront position, whereas in /ey/ it represents a shorter movement, which starts from either a lower mid [ɛ] or a higher mid [e] and does not usually go beyond the

Figure 3.1 Articulatory classification of English vowels.

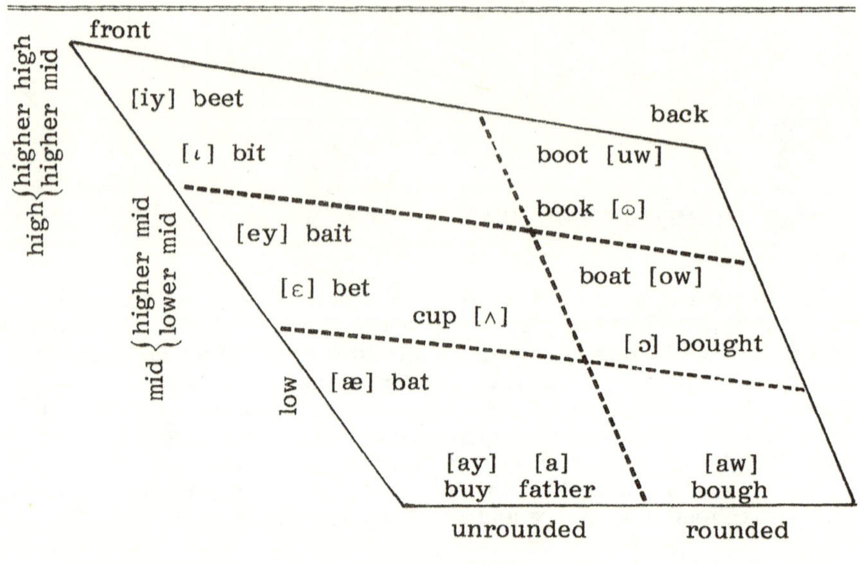

Figure 3.2 English diphthongs.

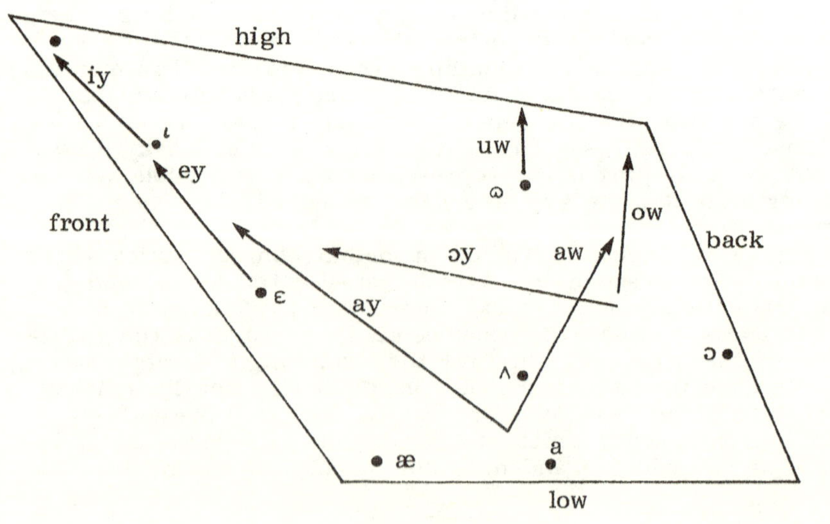

position of the lower high vowel [ι]. Likewise, the back upglide of [aw] is shorter than its counterpart in [ow], and in both [ay] and [aw] the point of departure is more fronted than in the single nucleus [a]. In the glided articulation of [iy] and [uw], the initial vowel is formed at about the level of a lower high [ι] and [ω], respectively. Figure 3.2, partly based on Ladefoged's diagram (1975:69), provides a visual illustration of these differences.

The simple nuclei in Figure 3.1 stand for single vowels and the complex ones for diphthongs. The functional contrast between simple vowels and diphthongs--that is, between simple and complex syllable nuclei--raises some problems of phonological interpretation. Kurath (1964:98ff.) points out that the vowels of *boat*, *bait*, *boot*, and *bee* occur as both monophthongs and diphthongs in American English. Both varieties of the high nuclei ([iy] and [uw] in Figure 3.1) coexist side by side, with the frequency of each type varying from one region to another. As to the mid nuclei ([ey] and [ow] in Figure 3.1), their most common manifestation takes the phonetic shape of upgliding diphthongs.

Regarding the distribution and phonetic properties of syllabic nuclei, Delattre (1965:55) has shown that 'in most American-English dialects, all vowels are more or less diphthongized.' He drew a convenient distinction between diphthongs and diphthongized vowels, by defining as diphthongs those vowels found in the nucleus of words like *fire* [ay], *shout* [aw], and *joy* [ɔy], 'in which a particular change of color is necessary for comprehension', and as diphthongized vowels those nuclei 'in which no particular change of color is indispensable for comprehension' (1965:94), as in *bait*, *goat*, *bat*, *bit*, *beet*, and *boot*. He also determined that the vowels of words like *know*, *Fay*, *do*, and *bee* are usually diphthongized, and that throughout their articulation they

> changent constamment de timbre ... l'articulation ... commence toujours par une phase surouverte des lèvres, des mâchoires et un peu moins de l'abaisement de la langue, et se termine par une phase surfermée. Ainsi la voyelle visée est atteinte indirectement, par le détour d'une voyelle plus ouverte (1966:102).[1]

The phonetic transcription of such diphthongized vowels would be as follows (Delattre 1965:68; 1966:Figures 1-4).

know [nnnɔɔɔɔow]
Fay [fffɛɛɛɛeeeey]
do [dddωωωuuuuw]
bee [bbbιιiiiy]

It would be possible to follow Chomsky and Halle (1968:50ff.) in postulating [+tense] vowels in the underlying representation of diphthongs. The derivation of phonetic diphthongs would be a consequence of phonological rules which would capture the relationships between complex nuclei and [-tense] vowels in pairs of words such as derive:derivative, grateful:gratitude, and so on. However, this procedure would be of limited use in a study such as the present one, which aims at comparing the vowels of two languages on the basis of actual contrasts manifested through their surface forms, rather than on the basis of abstract underlying phonemes.[2]

The phonological contrast between diphthongs and diphthongized vowels may be captured by postulating the complex nuclei /ay/, /aw/, and /ɔy/ in the underlying representation. However, the higher vs. lower contrast which obtains between the vowels of each set labelled [high] or [mid] in Figure 3.1 is not so easily disposed of. For one thing, it is apparent that the tripartite division of the dimension height is no longer sufficient, as there are five distinct height levels on either side of the scale (Figure 3.1). Furthermore, most complex nuclei have varying height, that is, their glide ends at a higher position than that of the vowel. One way to solve this difficulty would be to consider height a multivalued feature whose levels can be distinguished by integers rather than plus or minus signs, and to assign the value 1 to the lowest level, 2 to the next one, and so on (Ladefoged 1975:240; Sommerstein 1977:112). Since complex nuclei involve a transition from one height level to another, their height would be represented by a two-digit system. Thus, while [a] is [1 height], [ay] is [1-4 height], and in the latter case the second integer refers to the height of the high vowel which constitutes the target of the glide. The higher high nucleus [iy], in turn, would be either [4 height] or, somewhat redundantly, [4-4 height].

Alternatively, one might indicate, in the classification of complex nuclei, the actual height reached by the glide, as indicated approximately in Figure 3.2. Thus one would have the following classification.

[ay]: [1-3 height]
[ey]: [2-4 height]
[iy]: [3-4 height]
[aw]: [1-3 height]
[ɔy]: [2-3 height]
[ow]: [2-4 height]
[uw]: [3-4 height]

A simpler solution, adopted by Agard (1970) involves using the feature [tense], which sets apart two large classes of vowels in terms of their privileges of occurrence or the modifications they undergo in specific environments. Agard's system employs four distinctive features, namely, [tense], [high], [low], and [back]. These, together with the features

[+syllabic], [-consonantal], and [+sonorant], which are shared by all vowels, make it possible to put together a classificatory chart such as that of Figure 3.3. For the sake of easy visualization, and to facilitate comparison with Portuguese (Chapter 4), [+tense] vowels are indicated by a superposed macron.

Figure 3.3 Distinctive features of the English phonological syllabic nuclei.

	/ī	ɩ	ē	ɛ	æ	a	ʌ	ɔ̄	ō	ɷ	ū	ay	aw	ɔy/
[syllabic]	+	+	+	+	+	+	+	+	+	+	+	+	+	+
[consonantal]	–	–	–	–	–	–	–	–	–	–	–	–	–	–
[sonorant]	+	+	+	+	+	+	+	+	+	+	+	+	+	+
[tense]	+	–	+	–	–	–	–	+	+	–	+	0	0	0
[high]	+	+	–	–	–	–	–	–	–	+	+	1–3	1–3	2–3
[low]	–	–	–	–	+	+	–	+	–	–	–			
[back]	–	–	–	–	–	+	+	+	+	+	+	–	+	–

The feature [tense] is neutralized for the complex nuclei or diphthongs /ay aw ɔy/. All these have in common a first component characterized as [+low], [+back]; however, /aw/ differs from the other two in that its second element, /w/, is [+back] rather than [-back]. Furthermore, the contrast between the features [high] and [low] is also neutralized, since all three nuclei have a [+low], [-high] first component followed by a [-low], [+high] glide. The contrast between /ay/ and /ɔy/ depends fundamentally on the difference between their first components as regards degrees of the feature [height]. In the double-digit classification mentioned earlier, this would yield the contrast [1-3 height] for /ay/ as opposed to [2-3 height] for /ɔy/.

As Ladefoged (1975:73f.) points out, neutralization of the contrast between [+tense] and [-tense] vowels occurs in stressed open syllables, as well as in syllables closed by [r], [ŋ], and [ǯ]. The phonetic import of that loss of contrast is that the vowel is articulated as a sound intermediary between the [+tense] and [-tense] vowels involved. Thus, in <u>seer</u> the vowel may be closer to [iy] or to [ɩ], and this noncontrasting variation is ascribable to individual differences of pronunciation. Figure 3.4 summarizes these cases of neutralization.

3.2.1 Vowel reduction. All of the nuclei seen so far can occur in both stressed and unstressed syllables (Ladefoged 1975:72), particularly when a word is uttered in isolation. In ordinary connected speech, however, most nuclei can be reduced in unstressed position. Reduction is related to a variety of factors, such as rhythm, stress variation, and muscular tenseness of articulation, among others. Its auditory effect is a blurring of the specific phonetic quality of a sound due to the neutralization of the distinctive features which set apart

Figure 3.4 Neutralization of the contrast [+tense] vs. [-tense].

	/ī/	/ι/	/ē/	/ε/	/æ/	/ʌ/	/a/	/ɔ̄/	/ō/	/ū/	/ω/
-C$	seat	sit	sate	set	sat	suck	sot	sought	sewed	sooth	look
-$	see	–	say	–	–	–	ma	law	low	sue	–
-r$	seer		sayer				mar	more		moor	
-η$	ring		ginseng		bang	sung	gong		–	–	–
-š$	leash	dish	-	mesh	bash	plush	posh		–	–	bush

two or more vowels. In English, reduction involves centralization of articulation, accompanied by varying degrees of lowering of the tongue. It also involves a decrease in lip-rounding in the case of [+rounded] nuclei and a decrease of the degree of jaw opening for the [-high] vowels.

Phonetically, a reduced nucleus can be [ɩ], or the high central vowel [ɨ], but in most cases it is actualized as a centralized mid vowel represented as [ə].[3] Such a reduced vocalic sound may be accompanied by an off-glide. See examples in Figure 3.5.

Figure 3.5 Stressed, full unstressed, and reduced unstressed nuclei.

Nuclei	Stressed	Unstressed	Reduced
/ī/	Egypt	Egyptology	Egyptian
/ɩ/	activity	active	activate
/ē/	population	populate	populace
/ɛ/	dexterous; record(n.)	dexterity	record(v.)
/æ/	Pat	abstract(v.)	Patricia
/a/	object(n.)	objectivism	object(v.)
/ʌ/	suspect(n.)	sustentation	suspect(v.)
/ɔ̄/	install; Lawrence	lawrencium	installation
/ō/	relocate	location	relocation
/ū/	movement	cashew	...
/ω/	look	hussar	...
/ay/	minus	minute(adj.)	minutia
/aw/	outrage	outrageous	...
/ɔy/	boil	parboil	...

3.3 **Consonants.** The consonants of English can be described, from an articulatory viewpoint, by means of categories like those used for Portuguese (Figure 2.11), with some variation so as to account for articulations typical of English. Regarding the position of the articulators, the feature [interdental] is necessary to describe the initial fricatives of thin [θ] and that [ð]. There is also a new manner of articulation, namely, [affricate], required to classify the initial sounds of cheap [č] and jeep [ǰ]. Affricates are noncontinuant consonants, since in their articulation there is interruption of the airflow in the oral cavity. The other manner feature required is [glide], which serves to classify the sounds which occur initially in water [w], yod [y], home [h], and rat [r]. A general classification of English consonants is shown in Figure 3.6, and the phonological contrasts among them are illustrated by the examples in Figure 3.7.

The classification in Figure 3.6 is redundant, but by using a binary distinctive feature approach, as was done for

Figure 3.6 English consonants.

				Bilabial		Labiodental		Interdental		Alveolar		Alveopalatal		Dorsovelar		
				vl	vd	vl	vd	vl	vd	vl	vd	vl	vd	vl	vd	
Consonant	Noncontinuant	Non-nasal	Stop	p	b					t	d			k	g	Non-sonorant
			Affricate									ǰ	č			
		Nasal			m						n				ŋ	Sonorant
	Continuant	Fricative				f	v	θ	ð̌	s	z	š	ž			Non-sonorant
		Lateral									l					Sonorant
	Glide					y	w	r	h							

Figure 3.7 Consonantal contrasts.

	Initial	Medial	Final
/p/	pain	dapper	cap
/b/	bane	dabber	cab
/t/	tame	catty	cat
/d/	dame	caddy	cad
/č/	chest	riches	catch
/ǰ/	jest	ridges	cadge
/k/	kale	lacking	lack
/g/	gale	lagging	lag
/f/	fain	wafer	sheaf
/v/	vane	waiver	sheave
/θ/	thigh	ether	wreath
/ð/	thy	either	wreathe
/s/	sane	lacer	mace
/z/	Zane	laser	maze
/š/	Shane	mesher (leach)	ruche
/ž/	...	measure (leisure)	rouge
/m/	maim	gamely	dim
/n/	name	gainly	din
/ŋ/	...	ping	ding
/l/	lime	tiling	mile
/r/	rhyme	tiring	mire
/j/	yap	...	...
/w/	wet	...	...
/h/	hip	...	...

Portuguese (Figure 2.12), a nonredundant classification of English consonants is obtained, as shown in Figure 3.8. Those features can be organized in matrices, each of which defines a specific consonant, as shown in Figure 3.9. It should be noticed that the cooccurrence of the features [-consonantal] and [-syllabic] defines the glides [w] and [y], which are included in the inventory of underlying phonemes by virtue of the way they pattern in the language. Sounds classified as [-consonantal] and [+syllabic] are, of course, vowels. It is also apparent that, for [-continuant] sounds, one of the features [nasal] and [sonorant] is redundant, since their value coincides in all cases.

3.3.1 Phonetic realization of consonants. Like the vowels, the consonants vary in their phonetic realization according to the environment where they occur. In this section, the more important variants of that realization are analyzed.

3.3.1.1 Stops. The voiceless stops /p/, /t/, and /k/ have several features in common besides those used for their general articulatory classification. In syllable-initial position, particularly at the beginning of a word, they are articulated with audible aspiration, as in pan [p^hæn], tan [t^hæn], and can [k^hæn]. In absolute final position or before another

Figure 3.8 Distinctive features of English consonants.

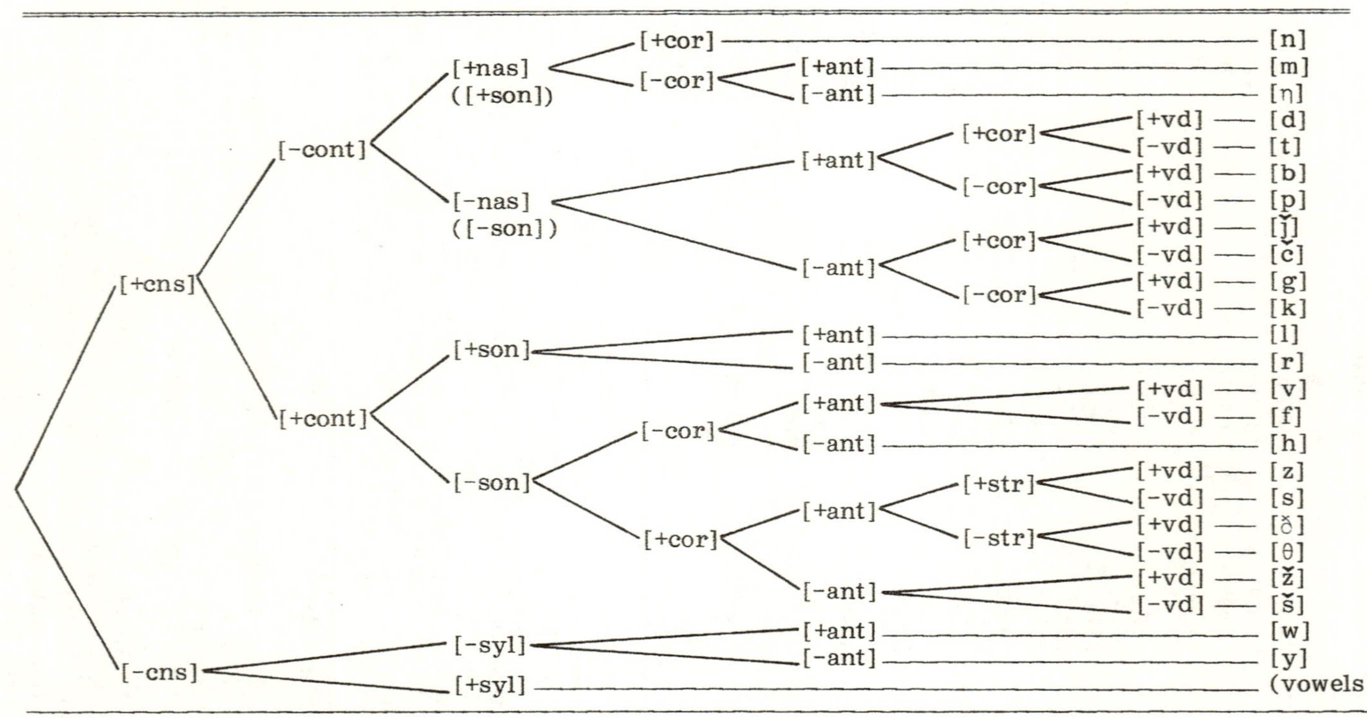

Figure 3.9 Feature specifications for English consonants.

	/p	b	t	d	k	g	m	n	ŋ	f	v	s	z	š	ž	θ	ð	č	ǰ	l	y	w	r	h/
consonantal	+	+	+	+	+	+	+	+	+	+	+	+	+	+	+	+	+	+	+	+	–	–	+	+
syllabic	–	–	–	–	–	–	–	–	–	–	–	–	–	–	–	–	–	–	–	–	–	–	–	–
sonorant	–	–	–	–	–	–	+	+	–	–	–	–	–	–	–	–	–	–	–	+	+	+	+	–
continuant	–	–	–	–	–	–	–	–	–	+	+	+	+	+	+	+	+	–	–	+	+	+	+	+
anterior	+	+	+	+	–	–	+	+	–	+	+	+	+	–	–	+	+	–	–	+	+	–	–	–
coronal	–	–	+	+	–	–	–	+	–	–	–	+	+	+	+	+	+	+	+	+	–	–	+	–
strident	–	–	–	–	–	–	–	–	–	–	–	+	+	+	+	–	–	+	+	–	–	–	–	–
nasal	–	–	–	–	–	–	+	+	+	–	–	–	–	–	–	–	–	–	–	–	–	–	–	–
glide	–	–	–	–	–	–	–	–	–	–	–	–	–	–	–	–	–	–	–	–	+	+	+	+
voiced	–	+	–	+	–	+	+	+	+	–	+	–	+	–	+	–	+	–	+	+	+	+	+	–

consonant, a stop is usually unreleased, as in lap [læp°], late [leyt°], or lab now ['læb°'naw] (as in Are you going to the lab now?). The voiced stops /b/, /d/, and /g/ are never aspirated. However, though not distinctive, aspiration does play a role in keeping voiceless consonants apart from their voiced homorganic counterparts, which tend not to be fully voiced before or after a pause.

The contrast between /t/ and /d/ is regularly neutralized in intervocalic post-stressed position, through voicing of /t/, which can be realized as an alveolar flap [ɾ], as in city ['sɪɾɨy], letting ['lɛɾɪŋ], and so on. Nevertheless, a contrast is partially kept, by some speakers at least, by articulating a short stressed vowel when the following stop is originally voiced in the underlying representation, as in kitty/kitties, which have a /t/ in the underlying representation, vs. kiddie/kiddies, which have a /d/. The relevant rule would be (3.1).

(3.1) $[+\text{syllabic}] \rightarrow [+\text{short}] \;/\; \underset{[+\text{stress}]}{\underline{\qquad}} \; /t/ \; [+\text{syl}] \; ([+\text{cns}])$

3.3.1.2 **Nasals.** Of the nasal consonants, only [ŋ] never occurs initially. Some authors (e.g. Bolinger 1975:81–82) prefer to leave it out of the phonological inventory and derive it from the underlying sequence /ng/. In this interpretation, the relevant rules would be as follows.

(3.2a) $\begin{bmatrix}+\text{cns}\\+\text{nas}\\+\text{ant}\\+\text{cor}\end{bmatrix} \rightarrow \begin{bmatrix}-\text{ant}\\-\text{cor}\end{bmatrix} \;/\; \underline{\quad} \begin{bmatrix}+\text{cns}\\-\text{ant}\\-\text{cor}\end{bmatrix}$

The other nasals, /m/ and /n/, present little variation. In some accents, they may be as shown in (3.2b).

(3.2b) $\begin{bmatrix}+\text{cns}\\-\text{ant}\\-\text{cor}\end{bmatrix} \rightarrow \emptyset \;/\; \begin{bmatrix}+\text{cns}\\+\text{nas}\end{bmatrix} \underline{\quad}$

Or they may have their specification changed by a rule like (3.3).

(3.3) $\begin{bmatrix}+\text{cns}\\+\text{nas}\end{bmatrix} \rightarrow [+\text{syl}] \;/\; \begin{bmatrix}+\text{cns}\\-\text{obst}\end{bmatrix} \underline{\quad} \; \$$

This means they become syllabic in word-final position, as in bison ['bayzn̩] or seism ['sayzm̩] (Ladegofed 1975:79). In the speech of some individuals, they may be relaxed or even deleted before a consonant, after nasalizing the preceding vowel, as in comfort ['kã^{m}fərt] ~ ['kãfərt].

3.3.1.3 **Fricatives.** Like voiceless stops, voiceless fricatives are generally shorter than their voiced counterparts in final position, but otherwise they show little variation. When initial or final, voiced fricatives are voiced during only part of their articulation, unless they are preceded or followed, as the case may be, by a voiced segment.

/f/:/v/ Normally articulated labiodentally, voiceless and voiced as in fat [fæt] and vat [væt], respectively, with minimal variation caused by the type of articulation of adjacent vowels.

/θ/:/ð/ Normally articulated interdentally, voiceless and voiced as in thick [θɩk] and then [ðɛn], respectively.

/s/:/z/ Normally articulated alveolarly, voiceless and voiced as in sip [sɩp] and zip [zɩp], respectively. The apex of the tongue touches the alveolar ridge and the blade touches the front part of the palate, so that the air flows through a groove formed lengthwise in the middle of the blade region.

/š/:/ž/ Normally articulated as laminoalveolar fricatives, as in ashes [æšɩz] and azure [æžər], respectively. The blade of the tongue touches the palate, farther back than for [s] and [z]. A certain amount of labialization may be noticeable.

The voiceless continuant /h/ is sometimes listed as a glottal voiceless fricative. From an articulatory viewpoint, it is formed by a stretch of egressive air made audible by friction created during its passage through the pharynx and the oral tract. It has been described as 'the voiceless counterpart of the following sound' (Ladefoged 1975:55), because during its formation the tongue assumes the position necessary for articulating the following vowel. However, it occurs voiced by assimilation if a voiced consonant precedes it, as in manhood (O'Connor 1973:144). It is classified among the consonants by virtue of its consonant-like patterning in the language.

3.3.1.4 **Affricates.** Like stops and fricatives, voiceless affricates tend to be shorter than their voiced counterparts in final position. From an articulatory viewpoint, the two English affricates [č] and [ǰ] can be considered sequences of an alveolar stop followed by an alveopalatal grooved fricative, that is, [tš] and [dž], respectively. Phonologically--that is, from a functional point of view--they are more appropriately considered individual units, /č/ and /ǰ/.

3.3.1.5 **Approximants.** This category includes the remaining phonemes /l/, /r/, /y/, and /w/. Their articulation involves a constriction of the oral tract, caused by a movement of the tongue toward a fixed articulation. However, that narrowing is not sufficient to produce the type of turbulence typical of fricatives, and on account of that articulatory movement these phonemes can all be assigned the feature [+glide] (O'Connor 1973:207). Since these phonemes are realized by sounds which have characteristics in common with consonants and vowels alike, their classification varies somewhat from one author to another. Those who use the features [consonantal] and [vocalic] list /l/ and /r/ as [+cns] and [+voc], and /y/ and /w/ as [-cns] and [-voc] (Chomsky and Halle 1968:176, Bolinger 1975:79). Those who use the features [syllabic] and [consonantal] list /l/ and /r/ as [-syl] and [+cns] and /y/ and /w/ as [-syl] and [-cns] (Sommerstein 1977:112).

The normal realization of /l/ in prevocalic position is the apicoalveolar lateral [l], formed with the apex touching the alveolae, so that air escapes laterally, while the body of the tongue assumes a position similar to that of the following vowel. After a vowel, particularly in syllable-final position, there is a secondary articulation formed by the dorsum of the tongue raised toward the velum, as in mall [mɔɫ].

Prevocalic /r/ is articulated with a movement of the tongue toward the rear of the oral cavity, with the apex retroflexed. The sides are more raised than the middle portion and the air escapes laterally as well as over the apex. In dialects which preserve /r/ after vowels ('r-ful' dialects), postvocalic /r/ is articulated with a lateral constriction of the tongue and a retraction of its body toward the back of the oral cavity, with the apex inactive (Kurath 1964:74). In 'r-less' dialects, that is, those without postvocalic /r/, intervocalic /r/ is articulated like the prevocalic variety described at the beginning of this paragraph.

Both /l/ and /r/ can be assigned the feature [+liquid], useful for accounting for the [+syllabic] value they assume in words like pedal ['pɛdl̩] or eraser ['ɩreysr̩]. The relevant rule would be Rule (3.4) (Ladefoged 1975:79).

(3.4) $\begin{bmatrix}+\text{cns}\\+\text{liq}\end{bmatrix} \rightarrow [+\text{syl}] \;/\; \text{C} \_\_\_ \#$

Since the same phenomenon involves the nasals /m/ and /n/, a more general rule (3.5) can be used to account for the occurrence of all four phonemes as syllable nuclei.

(3.5) $\begin{bmatrix}+\text{cns}\\+\text{son}\end{bmatrix} \rightarrow [+\text{syl}] \;/\; \text{C} \_\_\_ \#$

Despite its bilabial, lip-rounded articulation as [w], the glide /w/ is specified as [-anterior] on account of its velar component, since the dorsum of the tongue rises toward the velum. The glide /y/ is [+anterior], and articulated as [y] with the front of the tongue raised toward the palate. Both glides are formed by means of a continuous movement of the tongue toward the position of articulation of a following vowel, as in war [wɔr], yawl [yɔɫ], or away from that position, as in out [awt], ahoy [ə'hɔy].

3.4 Syllable types. If the syllable nucleus is represented by V and the different consonants by C, the syllable types of English are as shown in Figure 3.10.

Figure 3.10 English syllable types.

V	I	/ay/
CV	buy	/bay/
CCV	flea	/flī/
CCCV	spree	/sprī/
VC	is	/ιz/
VCC	ounce	/awns/
VCCC	urns	/ʌrnz/
VCCCC	bursts	/bʌrsts/
CVC	tap	/tæp/
CVCC	burn	/bʌrn/
CVCCC	sixth	/sιksθ/
CCV	bra	/bra/
CCVC	bras	/braz/
CCVCC	brags	/brægz/
CCVCCC	glimpse	/glιmps/
CCVCCCC	twelfths	/twɛlfθs/
CCCVC	split	/splιt/
CCCVCC	script	/skrιpt/
CCCVCCC	scripts	/skrιpts/
CCCVCCCC	strengths	/strɛŋkθs/

Figure 3.11 Occurrence of English consonants.

	Absolute initial	Medial	Syllable-final	Absolute final
/p/	pat	temporal	captain	cap
/b/	bat	cabal	obtrude	cap
/t/	tap	canteen	batman	cat
/d/	dab	candor	oddment	cad
/k/	cab	cancroid	lectern	crack
/g/	get	forget	pigment	dog
/m/	met	fragment	whimsey	rim
/n/	not	fornicate	syntax	sin
/ŋ/	...	...	sphincter	sing
/f/	fat	sophisticate	softer	laugh
/v/	vet	invert	pavement	love
/θ/	think	enthrall	mathematics	bath
/ð/	that	father	rhythmic	wreathe
/s/	sip	insinuate	dastard	pass
/z/	zap	desirable	gizmo	close (v.)
/š/	ship	insure	bashful	ash
/ž/	...	seizure	rouging	beige
/č/	chap	achieve	parchment	catch

Figure 3.11 (Continued).

	Absolute initial	Medial	Syllable-final	Absolute final
/ǰ/	jeep	ajar	management	barge
/h/	hot	vehicular	...	...
/l/	leap	alate	algebra	mall
/r/	rap	comrade	bargain	spar
/y/	yap	lagniappe*	...	...
/w/	wet	memoir*	...	...

*Medially in foreign loans only.

With regard to single consonants there are a few restrictions of occurrence. All except /ŋ/ and /ž/ can occur in word-initial position and at the end of a syllable all consonants but /h/ are possible, though the glides /y/ and /w/ occur only as nonsyllabic elements of diphthongs.[4] The examples of Figure 3.11 illustrate the possible cases. Consonant clusters are studied in Chapter 4, where they are compared with Portuguese clusters.

NOTES

1. Delattre's analysis leads naturally to distinguishing between diphthongs with homorganic glides, such as [ey], [ow], [uw], and [iy], and diphthongs with nonhomorganic glides, such as [ay], [aw], and [ɔy].

2. Chomsky and Halle's view on this matter is still a question of debate. It has been said (Agard 1970:36) that their system 'is far too complicated, far too ponderous an analysis. What we need [for a contrastive analysis] is a basis for characterizing the two systems which will (a) set in proper perspective the underlying similarities and differences between them and (b) square sufficiently, nonetheless, with general phonological theory at its present very controversial point of development'. For another dissenting view, see Kohler (1971).

3. According to Delattre (1965:55), 'about 90 percent of unstressed vowels turn to some sort of schwa (neutral vowel)'.

4. In another phonological analysis (Fries 1945; Trager and Smith 1951), the nonsyllabic element of a diphthong is a phonological vowel, and consequently, /y/ and /w/ occur only prevocally.

4

COMPARISON OF PHONOLOGICAL UNITS

4.1 Introduction. The present chapter undertakes a systematic comparison of the phonological units of English and Portuguese from two complementary viewpoints. First, the overall systems are compared, with attention paid to the distinctive features which enter into their composition, so as to highlight the most general similarities and differences. Second, there follows a point-by-point comparison which focuses on the similarities and contrasts between the phonetic manifestations of each phonological unit of L-1 and its counterpart in L-2.

The term 'counterpart' is used as an empirical means for facilitating comparison. Strictly speaking, a given phoneme of a given language, say English /v/, is to be considered a phonological unit on account of the relationships obtaining between it and the other units postulated in the phonological inventory of the language. Since the phonological system of a language is defined independently from that of any other language, contrasting two or more such systems requires a common basis that will justify any talk about similarities and differences between the two systems. Such a basis is provided by the description of both phonological systems in terms of the same inventory of distinctive features and phonological processes. Thus, since English /v/ is described by the same set of features used for describing Portuguese /v/, and since the phonetic manifestations of one are remarkably like those of the other, it can be said that Eng. /v/ is in fact the phonological counterpart of Ptg. /v/. This position is supported by the fact that a speaker of English learning Portuguese perceives Eng. [v] as being equivalent to Ptg. [v], an assumption borne out by his success in using the former sound when he utters Portuguese words with [v]. In so doing, he introduces into his budding phonological competence in Portuguese a phonological rule such as (4.1), whereby a set of phonological features is actualized as a labiodental voiced fricative sound.

(4.1) $$\begin{bmatrix} \text{+consonantal} \\ \text{-syllabic} \\ \text{-sonorant} \\ \text{+continuant} \\ \text{+anterior} \\ \text{-coronal} \\ \text{-nasal} \end{bmatrix} \rightarrow [\text{v}]$$

There is an element of gradience about any list of inter-language phonological counterparts. At one end of the list there are perfect or near perfect equivalents, such as English /v/ and Portuguese /v/. Near the opposite end of the spectrum are those units of L-2 which can be said to have only approximate counterparts in L-1. One such case is Ptg. /ṙ/ and /r̄/. While neither of these is an exact counterpart of Eng. /r/, the English speaker inevitably uses the latter as a first approximation to either Ptg. /ṙ/ or /r̄/. By so doing, he creates for himself a double problem. Phonologically, he overlooks the functional contrast between /ṙ/ and /r̄/, and phonetically, he introduces into his incipient competence in Portuguese a retroflexed articulation which is lacking in the standard varieties of that language. From the viewpoint of the contrastive analyst, the contrast between Eng. /r/ and Ptg. /ṙ/, /r̄/ constitutes a troublesome spot which interferes in the acquisition of native-like phonological competence in the latter language.[1] Furthermore, there are also phonological units in either language which have no counterpart in the other.

4.2 Portuguese vowels vs. English vowels. In order to facilitate the comparison, some minor adjustments have to be introduced in the classification of vowels presented earlier in Chapters 2 and 3. Leaving aside the English diphthongs /ay/, /aw/, and /ɔy/ for the time being, the vowel units of the two languages may be described in articulatory terms, as in Figure 4.1, or distinctive features, as in Figure 4.2.

Figure 4.1 Comparison of Portuguese and English vowels (articulatory terms).

Portuguese:				English:		
Front	Central	Back		Front	Central	Back
/i/		/u/	High	/ī/ /ɩ/		/ū/ /ω/
/e/		/o/	Mid	/ē/ /ɛ/	/ʌ/	/ō/
/ɛ/	/a/	/ɔ/	Low	/æ/	/a/	/ɔ/

Figure 4.2 Comparison of Portuguese and English vowels (distinctive features).

Portuguese:								English:										
i	e	ɛ	a	ɔ	o	u		i	ɩ	ē	ɛ	æ	a	ʌ	ɔ	ō	ɷ	ū
/	/	/	/	/	/	/	Tense	+	−	+	−	−	−	−	−	+	−	+
+	−	−	−	−	−	+	High	+	+	−	−	−	−	−	−	−	+	+
−	−	+	+	+	−	−	Low	−	−	−	−	+	+	−	+	−	−	−
+	+	+	−	−	−	−	Front	+	+	+	+	+	−	−	−	−	−	−
−	−	−	−	+	+	+	Back	−	−	−	−	−	−	−	+	+	+	+

Both systems may be reduced to three height degrees only, which means that Ptg. /a/ is now distinguished from either /ɛ/ or /ɔ/ as regards the horizontal position of the tongue alone (even though phonetically, [a] is lower than either [ɛ] or [ɔ]). Likewise, Eng. /a/ is defined as both [-front] and [-back] (which corresponds to the articulatory category of central), and it is thus opposed to the [+low] vowels [æ] and [ɔ], which are, respectively, [+front] and [+back]. The most important difference between the two schemata in Figure 4.2 is the feature [tense], which plays no role in Portuguese but is relevant for differentiating the English vowels /ī/, /ē/, /ū/ from, respectively, /ɩ/, /ɛ/, and /ɷ/, though it is redundant for the remaining vowels.

With regard to complex vowel nuclei, all Portuguese diphthongs can be regarded as deriving from vowel + vowel combinations under the conditions explained in Chapter 2; consequently, there is no need to postulate diphthongs in the underlying representation. The English diphthongized nuclei [iy], [ey], [ow], and [uw] derive from the [+tense] underlying simple vowels /ī/, /ē/, /ō/, and /ū/, while [aw], [ay], and [ɔy] are taken as being underlying diphthongs (Agard 1970:37f., Connor 1973:154). Since the glides /y/ and /w/ are part of the underlying inventory, those diphthongs might be alternatively considered phonological sequences of vowel + glide, or they might be considered as resulting from sequences of the type vowel + vowel in the same syllable (Abercrombie 1967:60). From the viewpoint of contrastive analysis, it is more important to pay attention to the similarities between surface Eng. [ay], [aw], [ɔy] and Ptg. [ay], [aw], [ɔy] than to split hairs about competing phonological descriptions.

4.3 Portuguese vowels and falling diphthongs vs. English syllable nuclei

4.3.1 Portuguese /i/ vs. English /ī/ and /ɩ/. Stressed Ptg. [i] is articulated somewhat higher and more fronted than Eng. [iy]. It is also shorter, lacking any trace of diphthongization. In unstressed position, it is somewhat lower and quite close to the lower high front English vowel [ɩ]. The opposition may be represented as in diagram (4.2).[2]

(4.2)

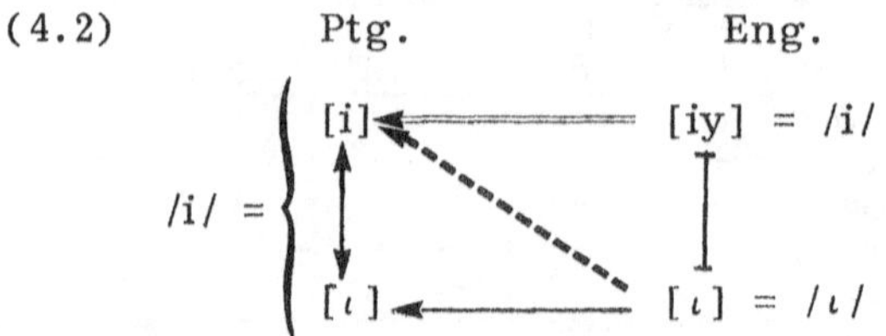

The subjects showed a tendency not only to use Eng. [iy] in open stressed syllables, as in aqui *[ə'kiy], but also to use Eng. [ɩ] in stressed closed syllables, as in vista *['vɩstə].[3] Although neither English syllable nucleus is a perfect substitute for Ptg. [i], Eng. [iy] will do as an adequate approximation, provided that its offglide is omitted (4.3a). Eng. [ɩ], however, will not do at all, as Ptg. [ɩ] may occur only in unstressed position (4.3b).

(4.3a)	Ptg. /i/ = [i]	Eng. /ī/ = [iy]
	pi	pee
	mi	me
	li	lee

(4.3b)	Ptg. /i/ = [ɩ]	Eng. /ɩ/ = [ɩ]
	mistura	mistique
	avisar	vista
	citar	sitar

(4.3c)	Ptg. /i/ = [i]	Eng. /ɩ/ = [ɩ]
	diz	this
	fiz	fizz
	giz	gizmo

4.3.2 Portuguese /e/, /ei/ vs. English /ē/. As diagram (4.4) indicates, there is in Portuguese a distinctive contrast between the single-vowel nucleus /e/ (phonetically [e]) and the two-vowel nucleus /ei/ (phonetically a diphthong, [ey]), as in dê vs. dei. The tense English vowel /ē/, in turn, is normally realized as a phonetic diphthong, [ey].

(4.4) Ptg. Eng.

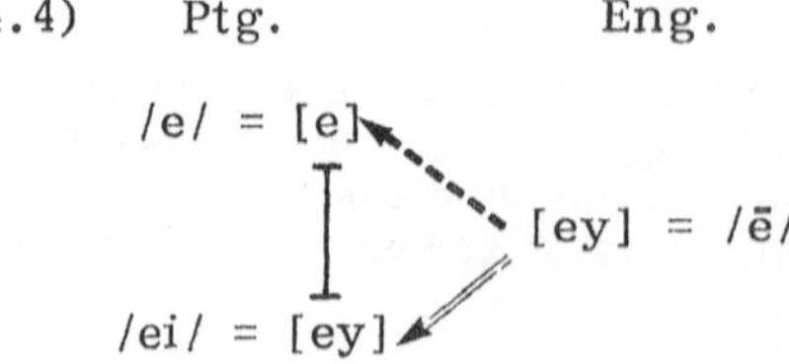

Ptg. /e/ is the only vowel in the general range of Eng. /ē/ and subjects consistently substituted the latter for the former, particularly in final stressed position, as in você *[vo'sey], porque *[pur'key]. This cancelled the contrast referred to, so that both dê and dei sounded like [dey]. Learners' difficulties are compounded by the fact that Ptg. /e/ tends to be slightly diphthongized in colloquial speech when followed by /s/ before pause. Thus, vez /ves/ is either [ves] or [ve^{y}s], fez /fes/ is either [fes] or [fe^{y}s], and so on. Eng. [ey] may be used whenever Portuguese presents either an underlying /ei/, as in (4.5a), or an underlying /es#/, as in (4.5b). Otherwise, Eng. [ey] serves only as a point of departure for the articulation of Ptg. [e], and always with the proviso that it be pronounced without an offglide.

(4.5a)	Ptg. /ei/ = [ey]	Eng. /ey/ = [ey]
	rei	ray
	sei	say
	dei	pay
	lei	lay

(4.5b)	Ptg. /e/ = [e]~[ey]	Eng. /ey/ = [ey]
	vez	vase
	fez	fays
	mês	maze
	rês	raise

4.3.3 **Portuguese /e/, /ɛ/ vs. English /ɛ/, /æ/.** In the range of front mid vowels, Portuguese offers a contrasting pair, /ɛ/ and /e/, whose members are farther apart than is the case with the English front vowels /ɛ/ and /æ/. Furthermore, Ptg. /e/, /ɛ/ are respectively higher than Eng. /ɛ/, /æ/. The opposition is shown in diagram (4.6).

(4.6) Ptg. Eng.

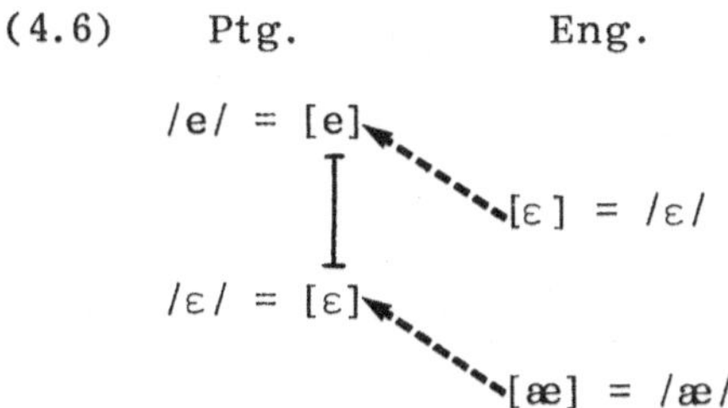

Subjects' efforts to avoid diphthongizing Ptg. /e/ in stressed position seemed related to their substitution of a lower mid vowel in the range of Eng. [ɛ] for Ptg. [e]. This entailed the mispronunciation of words such as vê *[vɛ] or rede *[xɛǰi], as well as the cancellation of contrasts such as este ['esti] vs. este '[ɛsti]. Having equated Ptg. /e/ with Eng. /ɛ/, subjects proceeded to equate Ptg. /ɛ/ with Eng. /æ/, as in perde *[pærǰi], veste *['væsči]. This tendency was successfully checked by focusing on Eng. /ɛ/ as a point of departure for the correct articulation of Ptg. /ɛ/ (4.7a), and by actively contrasting Ptg. /ɛ/ and Eng. /æ/ (4.7b).

(4.7a) Ptg. /ɛ/ = [ɛ]	Eng. /ɛ/ = [ɛ]
sete	set
fede	fed
pega	beg

(4.7b) Ptg. /ɛ/ = [ɛ]	Eng. /æ/ = [æ]
sete	sat
fede	fad
pega	bag

4.3.4 Portuguese /a/ vs. English /a/, /ʌ/. Although the sounds within the range of Eng. /a/ are usually articulated farther back than those within the normal range of Ptg. /a/, there is enough overlap between the two phonetic areas covered by those phonemes to make it feasible to use Eng. [a] as an approximation to Ptg. [a], in stressed position as in caso ['kazu] or in unstressed nonfinal position as in amigo [a'migu]. On the other hand, Eng. [ʌ] is quite close to the allophone of Ptg. /a/ (phonetically [ə], found either before a nasal consonant, as in chamo ['šəmu] or in final unstressed position, as in coma ['komə]. The oppositions between the two languages are shown in diagram (4.8) and examples of each case are contrasted in (4.9).

(4.8)

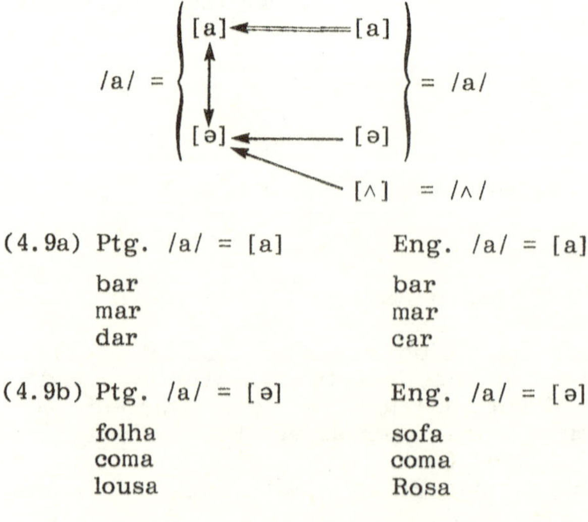

(4.9a) Ptg. /a/ = [a]	Eng. /a/ = [a]
bar	bar
mar	mar
dar	car

(4.9b) Ptg. /a/ = [ə]	Eng. /a/ = [ə]
folha	sofa
coma	coma
lousa	Rosa

(4.9c) Ptg. /a/ = [ə]	Eng. /ʌ/ = [ʌ]
boca	buck
loca	luck
moca	muck
pano	pun
dano	Dunn

4.3.5 **Portuguese /ai/, /au/ vs. English /ay/, /aw/.** In the two cases dealt with here, the phonological contrast involves the occurrence of two underlying vowels in the same syllable nucleus in Portuguese, as opposed to a complex syllable nucleus formed by a vowel and a glide in English. From a phonetic standpoint, there is very close correlation between Ptg. [ay] and [aw], on the one hand, and Eng. [ay] and [aw], on the other. In either case, the Portuguese phonetic vowel is more front than the English one; also, the offglide is shorter in the Portuguese diphthongs than in their English counterparts. As diagram (4.10) shows, the relationship between the two systems is straightforward, and Eng. [aw], [ay] are quite adequate as points of departure for the pronunciation of Ptg. [aw], [ay], as shown in (4.11). Some subjects showed a tendency to substitute Eng. [aɫ] (phonologically /al/) for Ptg. [aw] when this diphthong derived from the underlying sequence /al/, in words like sal.

Occurrence of velar [ɫ] instead of [w] is common in all cases of postvocalic /l/, evidently as a transfer from English. Although [ɫ] does occur in the speech of some Brazilians, there is no question that the more common articulation of postvocalic /l/ is currently [w], and many speakers tend to consider [ɫ] affected, for which reason learners had better avoid using it. This is a consequence of erroneous association of orthographic postvocalic l with the velar consonant [ɫ], as in Eng. pal, Sol, and so on (see Section 4.3.11).

(4.10) Ptg. Eng.

/ai/ = [ay] ◄════ [ay] = /ay/

/au/, /al/ } = [aw] ◄════ [aw] = /aw/

[aw] ◄- - - - [aɫ] = /al/

(4.11a) Ptg. /ai/ = [ay]	Eng. /ay/ = [ay]
vai	buy
sai	sigh
pai	pie

(4.11b) Ptg. /au/ = [aw]	Eng. /aw/ = [aw]
pau	powder
grau	grouch
cacau	bough

4.3.6 **Portuguese /ɔ/ vs. English /ɔ/.** As diagram (4.12) indicates, the relationship between these phonemes and their phonetic manifestations is straightforward. Ptg. [ɔ] is formed with the tongue higher in the oral cavity than is required for Eng. [ɔ], and it is also shorter. Otherwise, Eng. [ɔ] is as good an approximation to Ptg. [ɔ] as any. Subjects tended to pronounce Ptg. [ɔ] somewhat longer than is normal, particularly in open syllables, e.g. glória *['glɔ:rɩə]. For some speakers, such lengthening entailed the appearance of a short back glide, as in glória *['glɔ:ʷrɩə]. Comparisons such as those exemplified in (4.13) constitute a reliable point of departure for contrasting the sounds involved.

(4.12) Ptg. Eng.

/ɔ/ = [ɔ] ◄═══════ [ɔ] = /ɔ/

(4.13) Ptg. /ɔ/ = [ɔ]	Eng. /ɔ/ = [ɔ]
ló	law
só	saw
pó	paw
nó	gnaw

4.3.7 **Portuguese /o/, /ou/ vs. English /ō/.** The types of contrasts involved here are analogous to those which obtain between Ptg. /e/ and /ei/, on the one hand, and Eng. /ē/ on the other (see Section 4.3.2). The normal realization of Eng. /ō/, the phonetic diphthong [ow], can easily be substituted for Ptg. [ow] (phonologically a sequence of two vowels in the same syllable nucleus, /ou/), provided that its offglide is shortened somewhat. However, the contrast between Ptg. /o/ and /ou/ tends to be blurred in normal pronunciation through deletion of underlying unstressed /u/. This phenomenon is responsible for pronunciations such as estou [is'to] (instead of [is'tow]) and outro ['otru] (instead of ['owtru]). Diagram (4.14) summarizes these relationships.

(4.14) Ptg. Eng.

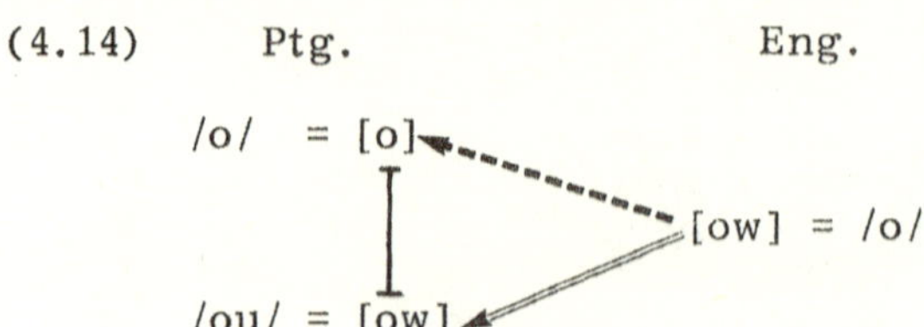

All subjects displayed a tendency to produce the diphthong [ow] instead of the single vowel [o] where only the latter was admissible, as in *recolha* *[r̄ə'kowl̃ə] or *rolha* *['xowl̃ə]. Once the contrast between Ptg. /o/:/ou/ has been learned, however, a tendency to produce [ow] where a phonological /ou/ exists leads some learners to acquire a somewhat artificial pronunciation, without the pronunciation of /ou/ as [o] which is widespread in native speech. Excessive emphasis on the contrast also seems to entail a kind of hypercorrection in which diphthongs are inserted where none should be, as in *correr* *[kow'xex] or *gozada* *[gow'zadə]. The items in (4.15) exemplify these different cases.

(4.15a) Ptg. /ou/ = [ow] ~ [o]	Eng. /ow/ = [ow]
sou	sew
dou	dough
loura	low
falou	fallow

(4.15b) Ptg. /o/ = [o]	Eng. /ow/ = [ow]
motor	motor
grosso	grocer
motel	motel
solar	solar

4.3.8 Portuguese /ɔi/, /oi/ vs. English /ɔy/; Portuguese /ɛi/, /ei/ vs. English /ē/. Diagrams (4.16) and (4.17) illustrate the contrasts involved in these two parallel cases.

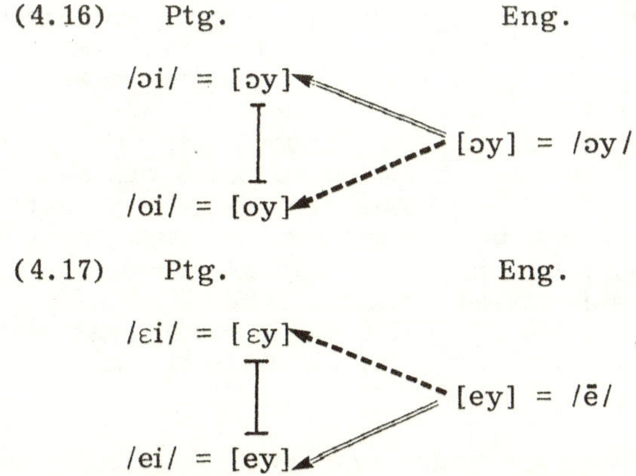

The main problem in both cases is caused by underdifferentiation between each higher mid vowel and its lower mid counterpart. Learners' tendency is to substitute for both elements of each pair of Portuguese diphthongs the corresponding English diphthong which, strictly speaking, serves as an approximation to only one of them. The errors recorded from the subjects included depois *[də'pɔys], foi *[fɔy], papéis *[pa'peys]. Sets of words exemplifying the relevant contrasts are given in (4.18).

(4.18a) Ptg. /oi/ = [oy]   Eng. /ɔy/ = [ɔy]

Ptg.	Eng.
boi	boy
goiano	goiter
pois	poise

(4.18b) Ptg. /ɛi/ = [ɛy]   Eng. /ē/ = [ey]

Ptg.	Eng.
réis	rays
méis	maize
fiéis	fays

4.3.9 Portuguese /u/ vs. English /ū/ and /ɷ/. This contrast parallels that between Portuguese /i/ and English /ī/, /ι/ (see Section 4.3.1). The relevant oppositions may be represented as in diagram (4.19).

(4.19) Ptg.   Eng.

/u/ = { [u] ← [uw] = /ū/
[ɷ] ← [ɷ] = /ɷ/ }

Stressed Ptg. [u] is articulated somewhat higher and more fronted than Eng. [uw]. It is also shorter, lacking any trace of diphthongization. In unstressed position it is somewhat lower and quite close to the lower high front English vowel [ɷ]. The subjects showed a tendency to use Eng. [uw] in open stressed syllables, as in rumo *['xuwmow], grude *['gruwǰi]. Use of [ɷ] in stressed closed syllables was also recorded, as in busto *['bɷstow], custa *['kɷstə]. Although neither English syllable nucleus is a perfect substitute for Ptg. [u], Eng. [uw] may be used as an approximation, as long as its offglide is suppressed. On the other hand, [ɷ] will not do in stressed position, since it occurs only unstressed in Portuguese. The examples in (4.20) illustrate the relevant contrasts.

(4.20a) Ptg. /u/ = [u]   Eng. /ū/ = [uw]

Ptg.	Eng.
Marilu	Marylou
lupa	loop
tabu	taboo

(4.20b) Ptg. /u/ = [ɷ]	Eng. /ɷ/ = [ɷ]
pular	pull
ocultar	bull
funil	full

(4.20c) Ptg. /u/ = [u]	Eng. /ɷ/ = [ɷ]
pus	puss
luz	look
cru	crook

4.3.10 Portuguese diphthongs without counterparts in English. The Portuguese diphthongs /iu/, /ui/, /eu/, and /ɛu/, listed with examples in (4.21), have no counterparts in English.

(4.21) /iu/ = [iw]	/ui/ = [uy]
viu	fui
faliu	cuida
mugiu	Rui
/eu/ = [ew]	/ɛu/ = [ɛw]
meu	céu
seu	léu
deu	chapéu

Regarding /iu/ and /ui/, a tendency was noticed for subjects to use a lower high vowel, [ι] or [ɷ], as the case might be, as the first element of the diphthong, thus originating pronunciations such as viu *[vιw] or fui *[fɷy].

There is a close parallel between the articulation of the diphthongs /eu/ and /ɛu/ and that of /ei/ and /ɛi/ (see Section 4.3.8). Mispronunciation can invariably be traced to underdifferentiation between Ptg. /e/ and /ɛ/. This, compounded by the error of equating Ptg. /e/ with Eng. /ē/, leads to substitution of Eng. /ɛ/ and /æ/, respectively, as the first element in Ptg. /eu/ and /ɛu/. Typical errors are seu *[sɛw] and céu *[sæw], the latter with the stressed vowel articulated with a degree of tongue lowering exceeding the limits of /ɛ/ for native speakers of Portuguese.

Another tendency, noticed for all four diphthongs considered here, consisted in pronouncing them as a sequence of two vowels: eu *['eu], chapéu *[ša'pɛu], viu *['vιu], cuida *['kɷɨdə].

4.3.11 Portuguese diphthongs formed by vowel + /l/. These diphthongs are formed through a process of realization of postvocalic /l/ as a backglide, [w]. An exhaustive list is provided in (4.22).

(4.22)		
cal	/kal/	[kaw]
mal	/mal/	[maw]
delgado	/delgado/	[dew'gadu]
Melgaço	/melgaso/	[mew'gasu]
Selma	/sɛlma/	['sɛwmə]
celta	/sɛlta/	['sɛwtə]
biltre	/biltre/	['biwtři]
Milton	/milton/	['miwtõ]
soldado	/soldado/	[sow'dadu]
folgado	/folgado/	[fow'gadu]
sol	/sɔl/	[sɔw]
arrebol	/ar̄ebɔl/	[ar̄e'bɔw]
culpa	/kulpa/	['kuwpə]
vulto	/vulto/	['vuwtu]

As was pointed out in Section 4.3.5, subjects tended to articulate postvocalic /l/ as [ɫ], velarizing it far more than would the minority of native speakers who use [ɫ]. While this is not a grave error, it does contribute to creating an accent which many, perhaps most, native speakers would consider less than desirable.

4.4 Portuguese rising diphthongs and triphthongs vs. English consonant + vowel or diphthong. It was seen in Section 2.4 that Portuguese rising diphthongs are unstable phonetic entities, easily decomposable into sequences of two vowels in contiguous syllables. To this type of Portuguese sequence of two phonological vowels forming one syllable nucleus, there corresponds in English a phonological sequence formed by a glide followed by a vowel. Figure 4.3 lists examples of the possible correspondences between the two languages.

Figure 4.3 Portuguese rising diphthongs and English counterparts.

Portuguese			English		
/ui/	[wi]	ajuizado	/wī/	[wiy]	we
/ue/	[we]	duetista	/wē/	[wey]	weigh
/uɛ/	[wɛ]	cueca	/wɛ/	[wɛ]	well
/ua/	[wa]	suavidade	/wa/	[wa]	wad
/uɔ/	[wɔ]	quota	/wɔ/	[wɔ]	water
/uo/	[wo]	duodeno	/wō/	[wow]	woe
/iu/	[yu]	miudeza	/yū/	[yuw]	ewe
/ie/	[ye]	piedade	/yē/	[yey]	Yale
/iɛ/	[yɛ]	biela	/yɛ/	[yɛ]	yellow
/ia/	[ya]	piabada	/ya/	[ya]	yah
/iɔ/	[yɔ]	idiota	/yɔ/	[yɔ]	yaw
/io/	[yo]	idiotice	/yo/	[yow]	yeoman

The diphthongized articulation of the Portuguese sequences in Figure 4.3 offers little difficulty to English speakers, who have at their disposal English sequences whose phonetic realization matches very closely that of their Portuguese counterparts. On the other hand, the articulation of those Portuguese sequences as hiatuses--admittedly a common solution, except when preceded by a velar consonant (cf. Figure 2.6)--presents some difficulties to English speakers. Since there are in English no sequences of vowels uninterrupted by a nonvocalic element (such as a consonant, or a semivowel, or a glottal stop), those hiatuses constitute an articulation problem with no counterpart in the learners' native competence. Consequently, the majority of learners' errors in this area involves inserting a separating element between the two vowels, usually a glottal stop or a glide, as the examples in (4.23) show.

(4.23a)	V ʔ V	(4.23b)	V y/w V
	juízo *[žuʔˈizu]		sueco *[suˈʔwæku]
	cuecas *[kuʔˈɛkəs]		diabo *[diˈʔyabu]
	Deodoro *[diʔoˈdɔru]		rua *[ˈxuwʔə]

As pointed out in Section 2.5, the only stable Portuguese triphthongs are those beginning with /u/ (phonetically [w]) preceded by a velar consonant (/k/ or /g/). Of those triphthongs listed in Figure 2.7, only two have counterparts in English; they are shown in (4.24).

(4.24) Ptg.		Eng.		
/uei/	[wey]	/wey/	[wey]	way
/uai/	[way]	/way/	[way]	(the letter) wye (y)

The pronunciation sample collected showed that subjects did not have any difficulty in articulating these Portuguese diphthongs, probably as a result of direct transfer of the pertinent rules in their competence in English. As in the case of falling diphthongs, however, a common albeit minor error consisted in making the offglide far shorter than is the norm in the pronunciation of native Brazilians.

4.5 Unstressed vowels. In the dialects of Portuguese taken into account in the present study, only the vowels /i/, /e/, /a/, /o/, and /u/ can occur unstressed.[4] From a phonetic standpoint, the possibilities of allophonic distribution vary according to whether the syllable considered is final or not. In nonfinal unstressed position, as was seen in Section 2.3.2, all those five vowels can occur in unreduced phonetic form, that is, [i], [e], [a], [o], and [u], respectively, and the phone [ə] occurs as an allophone of /a/ before a phonological nasal consonant. In final position, although [a], [o], and [e] are possible for contrast or emphasis, as a rule only [i], [u], and [ə] occur. This smaller phonetic inventory is easily interpreted as resulting from reduction of /e/ to /i/ and /o/ to /u/.

With regard to English, while it is possible for all vowels to occur in unstressed position (Ladefoged 1975: 72), the general tendency in ordinary speech is for them to occur in reduced form (Section 3.2.1), which annuls contrasts operative in stressed or unstressed but not reduced position. Diagram (4.25) compares the possibilities in both languages for unstressed vowel reduction.

(4.25)

Portuguese:					English:	
final		nonfinal				
[i]	[u]	[i]		[u]	[ɩ]	[ɨ]
[ə]		[e]	[ə]	[o]		[ə]
			[a]			

A tendency to reduce Portuguese unstressed vowels to [ə] or [ɨ] is generally noticeable in the speech of learners, with the consequent loss of most or all the contrasts among Portuguese unstressed vowels shown in (4.25). Among the instances of this widespread type of error, those shown in (4.26)-(4.30) were found.

(4.26) Loss of contrast between final /e/ (phonetically [i]) vs. /a/:

onde *['õdə] cf. onda ['õdə]
pegue *['pɛgə] cf. pega ['pɛgə]
case *['kazə] cf. casa ['kazə]

(4.27) Loss of contrast between final /u/ vs. /a/ with resulting loss of morphological contrast:

pelado *[pe'ladə] cf. pelada [pe'ladə]
mendigo *[mẽǰigə] cf. mendiga [mẽ'ǰigə]
estrago *[ɨs'tragə] cf. estraga [is'tragə]
arrebento *[ar̃e'bẽtə] cf. arrebenta [ar̃e'bẽtə]
falo *['falə] cf. fala ['falə]

(4.28) Loss of contrasts in nonfinal position:

/a/: /u/ usar *[ə'zar]
mudar *[mə'dar]
/a/: /o/ comprar *[kə̃'prar]
compra *[kə̃'prə]
colégio *[kə'lɛžiə]
/a/: /e/ beleza *[bə'leyzə]
pescaria *[pəskə'riə]
riqueza *[rɨy'keyzə]
cidade *[sə'daǰi]

(4.29) Use of [ɨ] for /a/ ([a] or [ə]):

ênfase *['ẽfɨzɨ]
banana *[bɨ'nənə]
semana *[sɨ'mənə]
fazenda *[fɨzẽndə]
fantástica *[fɨ̃'tastikə]

(4.30) Use of [ɨ] for /i/ or /e/:

menino *[mɨ'ninə]
Regina *[xɨ'žinə]
dezena *[dɨ'zenə]
descendo *[dɨ'sẽdə]
pegou *[pɨ'gow]
remédio *[xɨ'mɛdɨə]
recado *[xɨ'kadow]

4.6 Portuguese nasal vowels and diphthongs vs. English vowel + nasal consonant. Vowel nasalization in English results from the assimilation to a following nasal consonant,[5] a process analogous to the first case of nasalization in Portuguese described in Section 2.5. In both languages this is an automatic, nondistinctive process, which learners tend to transfer to their competence in Portuguese without any difficulty. Portuguese nasal syllable nuclei--simple vowels and diphthongs--such as those mentioned in Section 2.5 present a more serious learning problem. The phonetic differences between nasal nuclei and their nonnasal counterparts are obvious enough, and learners usually experience no difficulty in discriminating between the two sets. Correct production, however, is far harder. The commonest type of error consists in articulating a full nasal consonant next to the syllable nucleus, as in the instances cited in (4.31).

(4.31) lã *[lə̃n]
tem *[tẽỹn] ~ *[tẽỹm]
canta *['kãntə] ~ *['kə̃ntə]
pinto *['pĩntu]

When the incorrect nasal consonant is in word-final position it is usually linked to a following vowel, thus creating unlawful sequences such as those in (4.32).

(4.32) sem amigos *[sẽỹmə'migus̃]
com outro *[kõ'motru]
fin alegre *[fina'lɛgri]
sem esperança *[sĩnɨspərə̃nsə]

A common type of error involving diphthongs consists in imparting little or no nasalization to the syllable nucleus, which is thus underdifferentiated from its nonnasal counterpart, as in (4.33).

(4.33) mão *[maʔu] ~ *[maw^n] (cf. mau)
tem *[tɛʔi] ~ *[tey^n] (cf. lei)
dão *[daw^n]

4.7 Portuguese consonants vs. English consonants. It is convenient to begin the comparison of the consonant systems of English and Portuguese by examining the consonant charts of the two languages, as in Figure 4.4, which are condensed versions of those presented earlier (Figures 2.11 and 3.6), in the sense that they are reduced to a small number of articulatory features for the purpose of enhancing the similarities between the two systems.

Figure 4.4 Comparison of Portuguese and English consonants.

Portuguese consonants:

	[+anterior]		[-anterior]	
	labial	dento-alveolar	alveo-palatal	velar
Noncontinuant	p b	t d		k g
Fricative	f v	s z	š ž	(x)
Lateral		l	l	
Nasal	m	n	ñ	
Vibrant		ř r̄		

English consonants:

	[+anterior]		[-anterior]		
	labial	dento-alveolar	alveo-palatal	velar	glottal
Noncontinuant	p b	t d	č ǰ	k g	
Fricative					
-strident	f v	θ ð			h
+strident		s z	š ž		
Lateral		l			
Nasal	m	n		n	
Glide	w	r	y		

The feature [labial] applies to all phonemes whose articulation involves one or both lips. In either language, the contrast among the elements of the subset thus labeled is a function of manner of articulation, and within each division of this parameter it is a function of the feature [voiced].

There are three subsets of corresponding labial consonants in each language, that is, contrasting elements each of which contrasts with every other element in the entire consonant set and bears within the labial subsets the same relationship to each other in both English and Portuguese. Thus in either language the subset /p b/ is opposed to the other two by being [-continuant]; the subset /f v/ is opposed to the others by being [+fricative]; and the subset /m/ is characterized by the feature [+nasal]. The parallel between the two languages is schematically represented in diagram (4.34).

(4.34) Eng. Ptg.

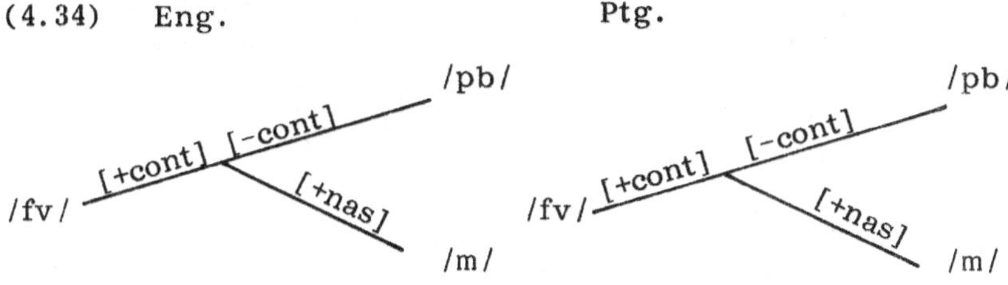

The place of articulation features [dental] and [alveolar] may be collapsed into a single category, namely, alveodental. In English, this category includes the five subsets /t d/, /l/, /n/, /θ ð/, and /s z/. In Portuguese, it includes the subsets /t d/, /l/, /n/, and /s z/. Each subset is distinguished from the others by the manner of articulation features [-continuant], [+lateral], [+nasal] and [+fricative]. Furthermore, a distinction is made between the [+strident] fricatives /s z/ and the [-strident] ones, /f v/ and /θ ð/. Here the parallel between the two languages holds only partially, as there are no units in Portuguese corresponding to English /θ ð/. In turn, Portuguese has the subset of [+vibrant] consonants, /ṙ r̄/, neither of which has a counterpart in English, since English /r/ is listed separately as a glide. The partial parallel between the two languages is schematically represented in diagram (4.35).

(4.35) Eng. Ptg.

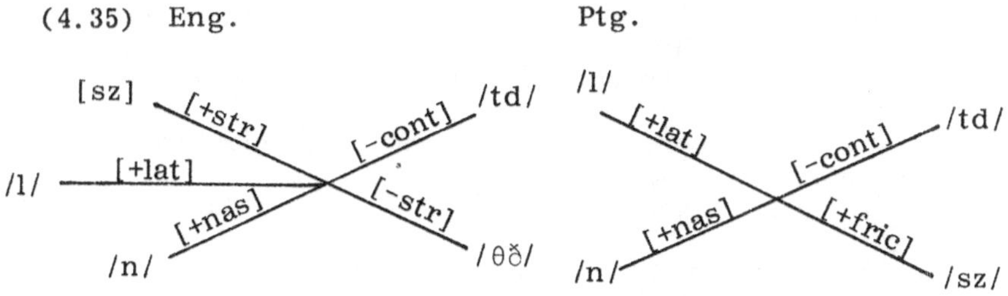

The remaining features of place of articulation, namely, [alveopalatal], [velar], and [glottal], may be subsumed in one single group, labeled [-anterior]. In English, the oppositions among the subsets within that group are defined by the manner of articulation features [-continuant], which includes the subsets /č ǰ/ and /k g/, kept apart by the plus and minus values, respectively, of the feature [coronal]; [+fricative], /š ž/; and [+nasal], /n/. The glottal fricative /h/ is included here because it is classified as [-anterior]; it differs from /k g č ǰ/

by virtue of being [+continuant], from /n/ as being [-nasal], and from /š ž/ as being [-coronal]. Here again, the parallel with Portuguese is imperfect, as this language lacks /č ǰ ŋ/ and includes the nasal palatal /ñ/ and the lateral palatal /l̃/, neither of which has a counterpart in English. Furthermore, dialects with one or another variety of velar 'strong r̲', that is, /x/, have yet another dimension, namely, [vibrant]. The partial parallel between the two languages is schematically represented in diagram (4.36).

(4.36) Eng.

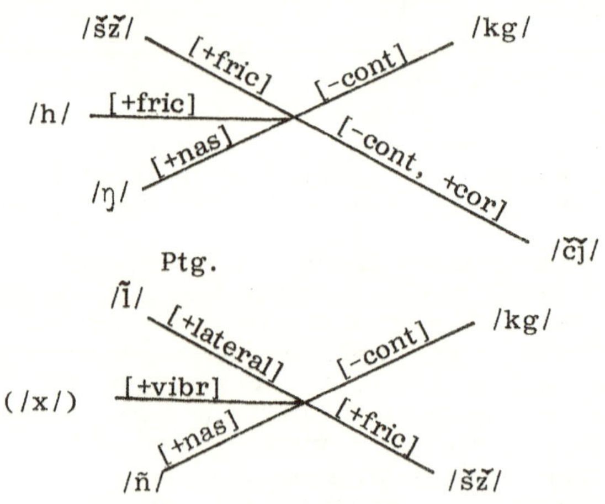

4.7.1 Comparison of consonantal phonemes. A systematic comparison of English and Portuguese consonants can now be undertaken, taking into account the following three categories, identified by their respective symbols in Figure 4.5:

(1) ○ : phonological units with practically identical counterparts in both languages;
(2) ☐: phonological units with close counterparts in either language;
(3) ⬚: phonological units of one language without a counterpart in the other.

4.7.1.1 Portuguese consonants with practically identical counterparts in English. Portuguese /f v š ž/ vs. English /f v š ž/. The phonetic manifestations of these consonants in either language are sufficiently similar to make positive transfer possible. The correspondences are direct, as shown in diagram (4.37).

Figure 4.5 Portuguese and English consonants: correspondences.

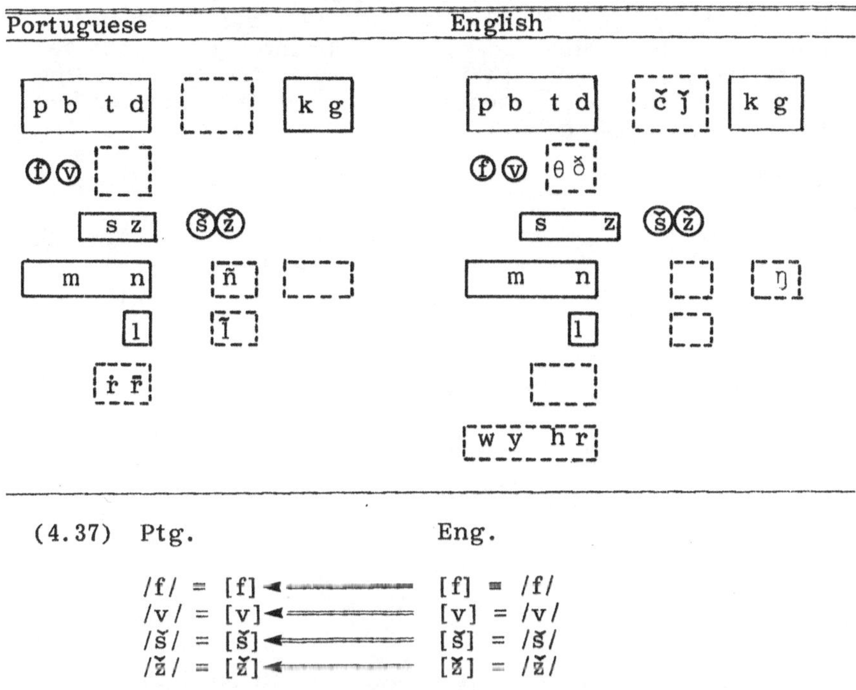

4.7.1.2 Portuguese consonants with close English counterparts but with important allophonic variations

4.7.1.2.1 Portuguese /p t k/ vs. English /p t k/. An important difference between voiceless stops in the two languages is the absence of aspiration in syllable-initial position in Portuguese. If carried over to this language, aspiration will cause an obvious foreign accent, without necessarily interfering with comprehension. Except for this detail, the articulation of Eng. /p/ and /k/ may be transferred directly into Portuguese. Although Ptg. /t/ is articulated as an alveodental consonant, while Eng. /t/ is fully alveolar, this difference has no significant ill effects, for either production or comprehension. Nor do learners have any difficulty in producing the affricate realization of /t/ before /i/, since Eng. /č/ can be used for this purpose. However, it has been noticed that some difficulty of comprehension is experienced, in the initial stages of exposure to Portuguese, at any rate, before the palatalization rule /t/ → [č] / _ /i/ is fully internalized by learners. This is particularly the case when fast speech is involved, due to the tendency of native speakers either to devoice or to drop altogether unstressed /i/ in that position, as in teatro [či'atrų] ~ ['čyatru] ~ ['$\check{c}_{\circ}^{y}$atřu] ~ ['čatřu] or *tapete* [ta'peči] ~ [ta'pe$\check{c}_{\circ}^{i}$] ~ [tapeč]. Some difficulty has also been noticed at the receptive level when learners are exposed to accents which use instead a prepalatalized affricate, [$t^{\check{s}}$], very common in Paulista, which English speakers tend to interpret as the sequence [ts], as in *tinha* ['$t^{\check{s}}$iñə], *retirado* [ře$t^{\check{s}}$i'řadu]. Diagram (4.38) illustrates schematically the correspondences involved in these phonemes.

(4.38) Ptg. Eng.

/p/ = [p] ← [p] } = /p/
[p] ⇠ [p^{h}]

/k/ = [k] ← [k] } = /k/
[k] ⇠ [k^{h}]

/t/ = { [t] ← [t] } = /t/
[t] ⇠ [t^{h}]
[$t^{\check{s}}$]
[č] ← [č] = /č/ }

4.7.1.2.2 **Portuguese /b d g/ vs. English /b d g/.** Most of what has been said about Portuguese /t/ applies, mutatis mutandis, to Portuguese /d/. English speakers have no difficulty in producing [ǰ] before /i/, as in *dia* [ǰiə], but some comprehension problems tend to occur, initially at any rate, in relation to prepalatalized [$d^{\check{z}}$], common in Paulista and Mineiro. Speakers who use the fully affricated variety of /d/ tend to devoice or drop unstressed /i/ in fast speech, so that words like *diabo* or *sede*, normally pronounced [ǰi'abu], ['seǰi] in slow and moderately fast speech may become, respectively, ['$\check{j}_{\circ}^{y}$abu], ['ǰabu] and ['se$\check{j}_{\circ}^{i}$], ['seč] (with devoicing of the consonant), and this tends to affect comprehension. Some difficulty at the receptive level has also been noticed in relation to accents (such as varieties of Paulista and Mineiro) in which a lesser degree of palatalization obtains, producing a prepalatalized affricate [$d^{\check{z}}$], which English speakers may interpret as the sequence [dz], as in *dia* ['dzia], *sede* [se'dzi].

English /b d g/ are not fully voiced except when preceded by a voiced segment, and the aspiration which accompanies initial /p t k/ serves to signal, more than voicing itself (Ladefoged 1975: 44–45), the contrast between the counterparts in voiceless/voiced pairs in the stop series. Absence of such voicing in Portuguese seems to be the factor responsible for learners' confusion, at the receptive level, between the elements of the Ptg. dyads /p b/, /t d/, and /k g/. Conversely, in Portuguese, voicing is an important factor in keeping apart those elements, and delayed onset of voicing, on the part of the English speaker, may erroneously signal the voiceless element to the ears of Portuguese speakers, since in this language voicing is the main factor in keeping apart those elements.

Diagram (4.39) illustrates schematically the correspondences and differences between /b d g/ in the two languages.

(4.39) Ptg. Eng.

/b/ = [b] ◄——— [b] = /b/

/d/ = { [d] ◄——— [d] = /d/
[dž]
[ǰ] ◄——— [ǰ] = /ǰ/ }

/g/ = [g] ◄——— [g] = /g/

4.7.1.2.3 Portuguese /m/, /n/ vs. English /m/, /n/. Interlanguage similarity between the phonetic realizations of each phoneme in prevocalic position is sufficiently great to make transfer of articulatory characteristics from L-1 to L-2 successful. In postvocalic, syllable-final position, although nasalization of the preceding syllable nucleus occurs in both languages, in Portuguese the nasal consonant is either deleted altogether or reduced to a brief consonantal constriction. The surface (phonetic) consequences of this process have been discussed in Section 2.5. Schematically, the interlanguage correspondence is shown in diagram (4.40).

(4.40) Ptg. Eng.

/m/ = { [m] / ___ V ◄——— [m] = /m/
$[^m]$ ~ ϕ / V ___ $ }

/n/ = { [n] / ___ V ◄——— [n] = /n/
$[^n]$ ~ ϕ / V ___ $ }

4.7.1.2.4 Portuguese /s z/ vs. English /s z/. There is enough similarity between the phonetic manifestations of Eng. /s z/ and their Portuguese counterparts in non-Carioca accents to make direct transfer successful, so that a learner's problems are limited to applying systematically the rule whereby syllable-final /s/ is voiced before a voiced consonant, that is, /s/ → [z] / ___ $ [+cns/+voice], as well as the rule whereby a word-final /s/ is voiced before any voiced segment, that is, /s/ → [z] / ___ # [+voice].

In Carioca, things are somewhat more complex, since final /s/ overlaps phonetically with /š/ before a voiceless consonant or a pause, with /ž/ before a voiced consonant, and with /z/ before a vowel.

(4.41) /s/ = [š]

malas ['maləš]
malas amarelas ['maləzama'řɛləš]
malas pretas ['maləš'přetəš]

/s/ = [ž]

malas verdes ['maləž'vexǰiš]

Diagram (4.42) shows the correspondences between Ptg. /s z/ and Eng. /s z/ in the dialects in question.

(4.42)

Carioca Ptg.			Eng.
/s/ =	[s]	←	[s] = /s/
	[ž]	←	[ž] = /ž/
	[š]	←	[š] = /š/
	[z]	←	[z] = /z/
/z/ =	[z]	←	[z] = /z/

Paulista and Mineiro Ptg.			Eng.
/s/ =	[s]	←	[s] = /s/
	[z]	←	[z] = /z/
/z/ =	[z]	←	[z] = /z/

4.7.1.2.5 Portuguese /l/ vs. English /l/. In prevocalic position, the realization of these phonemes differs phonetically in that Ptg. /l/ has a more anterior articulation, with the apex of the tongue touching the back of the front teeth and the blade on the alveolar ridge, while Eng. /l/ is articulated with the apex on the alveolar ridge. The difference is minimal and transfer of the English articulation amounts to but a slight foreign accent.

Postvocalically, Portuguese /l/ is articulated as a backglide [w] in ordinary speech, and English speakers should therefore learn to relate postvocalic /l/ to Eng. /w/. Furthermore, they must learn that [l] and [w] alternate freely between vowels over a word boundary, as in sal amargo [sawa'margu] or [sala'margu]. The correspondence diagram is shown in (4.43).

(4.43) Ptg. Eng.

```
        ⎧[l]   ◄══════════  [l] = /l/
/l/  =  ⎨ ↕                  I
        ⎩[w]   ◄══════════  [w] = /w/
```

4.7.1.3 Portuguese consonants without an English counterpart

4.7.1.3.1 Portuguese /l̃/ vs. English ϕ. The closest English approximation to Ptg. /l/ is the sequence /ly/. In fact, in colloquial varieties of Portuguese, there is a tendency to alternate [l̃] and [ly] in words such as malha ['mal̃ə], ['malyə] or ['malʸə], as well as words with underlying /l/ such as óleo ['ɔliu], ['ɔlyu] or ['ɔl̃u]. This tendency is probably reinforced by the relative rarity of minimal pairs contrasting /l/ and /l̃/.

Furthermore, in nonstandard accents (such as are found in Caipira dialects), [l̃] alternates with both [ly] and [y], as in calha ['kal̃ə], ['kalyə], or ['kayə]. These variants, however, are of limited value for the English speaker, for important as they may be to him at the receptive level, use of anything but [l̃] in any but the most informal styles connotes uneducated speech.

4.7.1.3.2 Portuguese /ñ/ vs. English ϕ. The closest English approximation to Ptg. /ñ/ is the sequence /ny/, as in Eng. canyon vs. Ptg. canhão. However, /ny/ cannot be used except as a point of departure toward the articulation of /ñ/, since pronouncing senhor or aranha, for example, as *[si'nyox], [a'ṙə̃nyə], while not necessarily interfering with communication, does impart a heavy foreign accent to the speaker.

4.7.1.3.3 Portuguese /r, r̄/ vs. English /r/. From a purely phonetic viewpoint, there would be good reasons for considering Ptg. /r, r̄/ as having no real counterparts in English. Structurally, however, as demonstrated by a large number of cognates, there is a close correspondence, although with a distribution that is entirely new to the English speaker. The two Portuguese phonemes contrast only intervocalically, but otherwise either they are in partial complementary distribution (only /r̄/ can occur initially or after another consonant) or then the contrast is neutralized, as when /ṙ/ in absolute final position is articulated as /r̄/.

English speakers have to learn the two-way distinction between /ṙ/ and /r̄/, besides the articulation of flapped [ṙ] and either trilled [r̄] or its velar/uvular homolog [x]. For /ṙ/, the closest approximation at their disposal in English is the flapped [ɾ] that occurs intervocalically in waiter, writer, etc., but this sound is not easily transferred. As for /x/, the closest English approximation is /h/, which serves only as a point of departure for acquisition of a velar or guttural trill.

(4.44)

initial [r̄]		intervocalic [ṙ]	
Roberto	Robert	Maria	Mary
Roma	Rome	área	area
rico	rich	histeria	hysteria
		espero	sparrow
		intervocalic [r̄]	
		arrogante	arrogant
		ferro	farrow
		garrote	garret
		burro	burrow
final [ṙ] ~ [r̄]		**postconsonantal [r̄]**	
mar	car	Israel	Israel
par	par		
por	for		

NOTES

1. The contrastive analysis presented in this chapter has been tested empirically against data found in the actual production of Portuguese by speakers of English. These subjects were graduate and undergraduate students at the University of California, Berkeley, with at least one full year of formal training in Portuguese.

2. The symbols used in the diagrams in this section are:

x ══► y	x may be used as an approximation for y in all or most cases or positions.
x ──► y	x may be used for y only in certain specific positions.
x - - - -► y	x tends to be incorrectly used for y by speakers of L-1.
x ◄──► y	x and y are functionally related/members of the same set/allophones of the same phoneme.
x ├──┤ y	x and y contrast functionally.
/x/ = [y]	[y] is a phonetic manifestation of the phonological unit /x/.

3. Examples of incorrect pronunciation are listed as originally transcribed.

4. In other dialects, such as those spoken in areas of the Brazilian northeast, /ɛ/ and /ɔ/ may also occur in unstressed position, as in Recife [xɛ'sifi] and Olavo [ɔ'lavu].

5. In both languages, the possibility of nasalization of a vowel by a preceding consonant is minimal and of no interest to this study.

5

COMPARISON OF PHONOLOGICAL SEQUENCES

5.1 **Introduction.** The contrastive analysis of individual phonological units given in the preceding chapter is complemented in the present one by a comparison of Portuguese and English sequences of phonemes and their phonetic results. The following headings are considered: (1) transition phenomena, (2) vowel sequences, (3) consonant sequences, and (4) consonant + vowel sequences.

5.2 **Transition phenomena.** The processes that take place in the transition of the articulation of a sound to the following one, either within the same syllable or over a syllable boundary, may be grouped into three categories: (1) disjuncture, (2) smooth or close juncture, and (3) open juncture.

Disjuncture (also referred to as internal open juncture) is a general label covering a variety of phonetic processes which signal the transition from one sound to the next or from one syllable to the next. It is disjuncture that accounts for the perceptual difference between English minimal pairs such as a nice house vs. an ice house, which are otherwise made up of the same phonological units. Disjuncture is traditionally represented by the symbol +, so a nice house would be transcribed /ey + nays + haus/, whereas an ice house would be /æn + ays + haus/.

Native speakers of English sometimes perceive such contrasts in terms of syllable division (Hill 1958:25), or they may relate them to the position of what they perceive as a slight pause between two words. In fact, most of the time there is no such pause, and the difference between the two phrases is actually related to the presence of a morphological boundary which causes the contiguous phonemes to be actualized as different allophones in each case (O'Connor 1973:225). Thus in an ice house, the final n is somewhat longer than its initial counterpart in nice, while the vowel is longer in the article a than in its allomorph an.

Absence of disjuncture accounts for smooth or close juncture. In this type of transition the passage from one sound to the next is effected without either an audible pause or any allophonic modification that might signal a difference between two otherwise identical sound sequences. This is typically the case of hiatuses in Portuguese.

Open juncture, finally, has been characterized as a 'kind of audible pause that comes at the end of a breath group after a terminal contour' (Agard and Di Pietro 1965: 44). It differs positionally from both disjuncture and smooth juncture, which occur between phonemes, rather than in final position. In both Portuguese and English, open juncture occurs at the end of utterances or, somewhat exceptionally, when a pause is required during an utterance, as after each item in a list or enumeration (as, for example, in a countdown).

In Portuguese, absence of disjuncture causes the sounds of a sequence like <u>a guarda</u> to be phonetically very similar to those in the verb form <u>aguarda</u>. This does not mean, however, that such sequences are absolutely identical.

As shown by Câmara (1970: 266ff.), variation in degrees of stress in Portuguese can play a role similar to that of disjuncture in English. There are in Portuguese two phonologically relevant degrees of stress, namely, strong and weak (a distinction sometimes referred to in terms of stressed and unstressed syllables, respectively). At the subphonological level, however, four levels can be distinguished, symbolized as 0 - 1 - 2 - 3, from weakest to strongest.

Degrees 3 and 2 correspond to strong stress. In words pronounced in isolation, strong stress is always 3; within the same breath group, however, only one word has stress 3, and all the other stressed syllables are reduced to level 2. Likewise, stress levels 0 and 1 correspond to subphonological variations of weak stress: level 1 occurs pretonically and level 0 occurs in posttonic position, as in the examples in (5.1).

```
(5.1) lá
       3

      lá vai
       2  3

      lá vai ela
       2  2  3 0

      lá vai Maricota
       2  2   1 1 3 0
```

Câmara (1970: 27) pointed out that it is such variation

> that makes it possible, at least in the case of normal Brazilian pronunciation, to distinguish homophonemic sequences of the type <u>celebridade</u> from sequences of the type <u>célebre idade</u> ... In the second expression the initial

vowel of idade merges with the final vowel of célebre, the minimum stress of the latter being maintained:

```
/selebridadi/  (celebridade)
 1 1  1 3 0

/selebridadi/  (célebre idade)
 2 0  0 3 0
```

For some speakers, Câmara's examples are not exactly homophonemic, since the first vowel of célebre, even with reduced stress level 2, is [ε] rather than [e], as in celebridade. The principle, however, holds for a number of other examples, such as those in (5.2).

```
(5.2) extraordinário[1]   extra-ordinário
      1   11  1 3 00     2   0 1  1 3 00

      Rosalinda          rosa linda
       1 13  0            2 0  3  0

      furacão            fura cão
       1 1  3             2 0  3

      matacão            mata cão
       1 1  3             2 0  3
```

This type of variation in stress level, just like disjuncture in English, can be a subtle device for word plays. An instance of this is found in the first lines of Mário de Oliveira's poem Fórmula 1.[2]

A pista é toda sua
é sua a cidade
feroz cidade
voraz cidade
veloz cidade

where the contrasts in (5.3) can be noted.

```
(5.3) feroz cidade  vs.  ferocidade
       1 2   1 3 0        1 1 1 3 0

      voraz cidade  vs.  voracidade
       1 2   1 3 0        1 1 1 3 0

      veloz cidade  vs.  velocidade
       12    1 3 0        1 1 1 3 0
```

Similar contrasts form the basis of puns, such as those in (5.4).

(5.4)	quero uma beladona[3] 2 0 1 0 1 1 3 0	vs.	quero uma bela dona 2 0 1 0 2 0 3 0
	viela 1 3 0	vs.	vi ela 2 3 0
	procurador 1 1 1 3	vs.	procura dor 1 2 0 3
	contadores 1 1 3 0	vs.	conta dores 2 0 3 0
	uma vagabunda 1 0 1 1 3 0	vs.	uma vaga bunda 1 0 2 0 3 0
	viravolta 1 1 3 0	vs.	vir a volta 2 0 3 0
	armarinho 1 1 3 0	vs.	ar marinho 2 1 3 0

5.3 Vowel sequences. Vowel sequences occurring in the same syllable were studied as diphthongs in Chapter 4. The occurence of two vowels in adjacent syllables (that is, separated by a syllable barrier in the underlying structure) originates a hiatus, as in Ptg. caolho or meandro. In such cases the transition from one vowel to the next is smooth, without any pause or interruption. In English, such sequences are interrupted by a semivowel, a consonant, a glottal stop, or juncture. A hiatus in Portuguese is a sequence of linked vowels in which each sound retains its phonetic characteristics while remaining as a separate syllable nucleus. All subjects examined showed a tendency to introduce a separating element--more often than not a glottal stop--between those vowels, thus creating incorrect sequences such as *[kaʔ'ol̃u] and *[meʔ'ə̃dṙu] instead of [ka'ol̃u] and [me'ə̃dṙu].

Hiatuses are most stable when one of the vowels is stressed and the unstressed vowel is /a/, as in maestro, caolho, ataúde, or Aílton. If both vowels are unstressed, there is a strong tendency, particularly in fast pronunciation, for the hiatus to become a diphthong. This is easily accomplished if one of the vowels is either /i/ or /u/, as in (5.5).

(5.5) rainhazinha [r̄a-i-ña-'zĩ-ña] ~ [r̄ay-ña-'zĩ-ña]
reunido [r̄e-u-'ni-du] ~ [r̄ew-'ni-du]
pátria ['pa-tṙi-ə] ~ ['pa-tṙyə]

If neither unstressed /i/ nor /u/ is present, a diphthong can still be formed. The first step is a process of synalepha whereby the syllable boundary is deleted, so that the two adjacent vowels occur in the same syllable. Then there is raising of unstressed /e/ and /o/, which are actualized as [i] and [u], respectively. This makes possible the application of the diphthongization rule which causes the raised vowel to be realized as a phonetic glide. Schematically, the process would be as in (5.6).

(5.6) underlying form: /ko-a-l̃a-da/
synalepha: /koa-l̃a-da/
raising of unstressed /o/ → /u/: /kua̯-l̃a-da/
diphthongization of /u/ → [w]: /kwa-l̃a-da/
raising of final /a/ → [ə]: /kwa-l̃a-də/
phonetic output: [kwa'l̃adə]

Other examples produced by the subjects were those shown in (5.7).

(5.7) aeronáutica: /a-e-ṙo-nau-tica/ → /ae-ṙo-nau-ti-ka/ → /ai-ṙo-nau-ti-ka/ → [ay-ṙo-'naw-ti-ka]
maometano: /ma-o-me-ta-no/ → /mao-me-ta-no/ → /mau-me-ta-no/ → [maw-me-'tə-nu]
meandroso: /me-an-dṙo-zo/ → /mean-dṙo-zo/ → /mian-dṙo-zo/ → [myə̃-'dṙo-zu]

When two vowels occur next to each other over a word boundary, several solutions are possible. They may be linked, forming a hiatus, as in aqui esta [a-ki-'ɛs-tə]; they may be fused, forming a diphthong, as in casa estranha [ka-zəys-tṙə-ñə]; or one of them may be eliminated altogether, as in cara honesto [ka-ṙo'nɛs-tu].

Across a word boundary, hiatuses are most stable when both vowels are stressed. See the examples in (5.8).

(5.8) vê ela ['ve-'ɛ-lə]
está essa [es-'ta-'ɛ-sə]
urubu ávido [u-ṙu-'bu-'a-vi-du]
Vovô Índio [vo-'vo-'ĩ-di-u]
até hoje [a-'tɛ-'o-ži]

Presence of an unstressed high vowel may originate a diphthong, as in (5.9).

(5.9) você espera [vo-'seys-'pɛ-ṙə]
lá estava ele ['lays-'ta-və-'e-li]
o Jacó urrava [u-ža-'kɔw-r̃a-və]
faço horrores ['fa-swo-'r̃o-ṙis]
caso acontecido ['ka-zwa-kõ-ti-'si-du]
mate azedo ['ma-čya-'ze-du]

The transition between two identical vowels may be fast enough to make the phonetic output sound like a somewhat lengthened vowel, as in (5.10).

(5.10) lá há muitos ['la-'a-'mũỹ-tus] ~ ['la:-'mũỹ-tus]
acho humilde ['a-šu-u-'miw-di] ~ ['a-šu:-'miw-di]
onde está ['õ-di-is-'ta] ~ [õ-di:s-'ta]

Unstressed /a i u/ may be eliminated before another vowel, as shown in (5.11).

(5.11) compra esse mesmo ['kõ-pře-si-'mez-mu]
fala essas coisas ['fa-lɛ-səs-'koy-zəs]
não fala isso não [nũ-'fa-li-su-'nə̃w̃]
pega homem a laço ['pɛ-gɔ-mya-'la-su]
manda uma só ['mə̃-du-mə-sɔ]
compre essa aí ['kõ-'přɛ-sa-'i]
de humanidade [du-ma-ni-'da-di]
quando é o jogo ['kwə̃-'dɛ-u-'žo-gu]
compro orégano ['kõ-pro-'řɛ-gə-nu]

In the analysis of the subjects' speech there was noticed a strong tendency to introduce a kind of disjuncture between vowels in contiguous syllables. More often than not, this implied disrupting a V-V sequence by means of a glottal stop, as in vi ele hoje *[viˀ'eliˀoži] or se ela é americana *[siˀ'ɛləˀ'ɛˀəmeři'kənə]. Disjuncture was also apparent between consonants in adjacent words, contributing to an undesirable staccato effect, as in automóveis baratos *[awto'mɔveys + ba'řatus] or usar sapatos *[u'zax + sa'patus]. This tendency also manifested itself when unstressed vowels were involved, thus preventing diphthongization, lengthening, or vowel deletion of the types exemplified in (5.9)-(5.11), e.g. você espera *[vo'seˀis'pɛrə], lá há muitos *[laˀaˀ'mũỹtus], or manda uma só *['mə̃dəˀ'umə'sɔ]. Elimination of unstressed /a/, /i/, and /u/ before another vowel, as shown in (5.11), seems particularly hard to incorporate into active use. It is possible that, for some subjects at least, this problem resulted from an effort to use a kind of spelling pronunciation mistakenly associated with correctness.

5.4 Consonant sequences. The number of possible consonant sequences in Portuguese is limited, and the ones that hold more interest for us are those that form cohesive clusters within the same syllable.

In the prenuclear clusters of the general type CC (where the consonants are necessarily different from each other, since there are no sequences or clusters of identical consonants in Portuguese), the first consonant is a nonnasal obstruent (/p/, /b/, /t/, /d/, /k/, or /g/) or a labiodental nonsonorant, that is, fricative (/f/ or /v/), and the other can be only either the anterior lateral /l/ or the flap /ř/. There are some cooccurrence restrictions. (1) There is no */dl/ cluster, except marginally in foreign lexical items and derivatives, such as Adler and adleriano. In the compound form adligar, the syllable boundary occurs between /d/ and /l/. (2) In absolute initial position, /vr/, /tl/, and /vl/ are very rare. (3) The cluster /vl/ appears initially only in the foreign name Vladimir and medially in marginal borrowings, such as the trademark Revlon [r̄e'vlõ].

In English it is possible to distinguish two broad categories of prenuclear clusters. First, there are those formed by /s/ followed by either a noncontinuant (spite, stall) or a labial fricative (svelte, sphere), or a glide (slide, sweet). These clusters have no structural counterpart in Portuguese and consequently are not of interest here. The second class comprises clusters beginning with a consonant other than /s/, and it includes homologs of most of the Portuguese prenuclear clusters. Initially, /dl/, /tl/, /vl/, and /vr/ do not occur, except in foreign loans such as Tlingit or Vladimir, or in onomatopoetic items such as vroom. Nor do these consonants occur medially as clusters, since in words like atlas, Adler, Revlon, or chevron the syllable boundary falls between the first consonant and the second. Figure 5.1 offers a comparative list of prenuclear clusters in the two languages.

Figure 5.1 Prenuclear consonant clusters.

	Initial		Medial	
	Ptg.	Eng.	Ptg.	Eng.
pl	planeta	planet	réplica	reply
pr	prazo	prize	compra	repress
bl	bloco	block	rublo	ruble
br	brinco	brink	abraço	abroad
tl	tlintar	Tlingit	atlas	...
tr	trama	tram	atrás	extract
dl	...	...	adleriano	...
dr	dragão	dragon	adro	adrenal
kl	clarim	clarion	eclesiástico	exclude
kr	crime	crime	recreio	excrete
gl	glosa	gloss	sigla	ogle
gr	groselha	grow	regra	aggressive
fl	flauta	flute	rifle	reflect
fr	francês	frank	africano	afraid
vl	Vladimir	Vladimir	...	...
vr	Vru*	...	lavra	...

*The feminine nickname Vru is the only instance of initial /vr-/ in Portuguese of which I am aware. In nonstandard dialects in which there is neutralization of the contrast between /l/ and /r/, Vladimir can be heard as [vɾadi'mi].

None of the Portuguese clusters in Figure 5.1 present specific difficulty to learners. Errors detected in the subjects' speech were of types also found in individual consonants, such as aspiration of initial /p/ and /k/ in words like planeta or claro. It was also noticed that subjects who normally pronounced Eng.

/r/ in a fricativized manner (phonetically [ɹ̥], as in *crash* [k^{h}ɹ̥æš] or *price* [p^{h}ɹ̥ays]) normally transferred that pronunciation to Portuguese, as in *prazo* ['p^{h}ɹ̥azu] or *treze* ['t^{h}ɹ̥ezi].

In the coda, the only frequent phonological consonant sequence in Portuguese is /ns/. Here, however, after nasalization of the preceding vowel, the nasal consonant /n/ is deleted, barely leaving a phonetic trace, as in the plurals *sons*, *bons*, and the prefix *trans-* (*transcrever*, *transpor*). Other possible sequences, all of low frequency, are /ls/ and /ṙs/. The former occurs only in *solstício* (phonetically [sows'tisiu]), and the latter in compounds that include the prefixes *per-* or *inter-*, such as *perscrutar*, *perspicaz*, and *interstício* (Cintra 1978: 81). Syllable division in the case of /rs/ + consonant is problematic. Head (1964:213) shows that in Carioca it can occur either before or after the fricative, that is, /...r-sp.../ or /...rs-p.../. Cintra's analysis (1978) of Paulista lists /-rs/ as postnuclear sequences, but my research indicates that in that dialect, as well as in Mineiro, either type of division is possible. The controlling factor seems to be primarily stylistic: in slow, careful speech, /rs/ is a syllable-final cluster, but in fast, relaxed speech the syllable boundary may come between /r/ and /s/. Each solution originates an additional, albeit marginal consonant sequence, that is, either final /-rs/ or syllable-initial (but not absolute initial) /sp-/.

There are also in Portuguese initial or medial consonant sequences found only in learned or borrowed words, in which there may appear the fricative /f/ followed by /t/ or a stop followed by a fricative or another obstruent, nasal or not. Examples are shown in Figure 5.2. In very careful pronunciation, such sequences form clusters initially, and medially they belong to adjacent syllables. In ordinary language, however, a front vowel, phonologically /e/ or /i/ (Câmara 1953:79), is inserted between the consonants, forming a syllable with the first. If stress falls before that consonant sequence, as in *técnico* or *óbvio*, insertion of the vowel creates a stress pattern, that is, words stressed on the fourth from last syllable: ['tɛ-ki-ni-ku], ['ɔ-bi-vi-u] (Câmara 1968; 1970:47). The phonetic realization of the inserted vowel can be [e], [i] or a reduced and lower, sometimes devoiced variant of a high front vowel ([ɪ] or [ɪ̥]). In dialects in which palatalization of dental stops takes place, a preceding /t/ or /d/ is affricated, as in *advogado*: [aǰivo'gadu], [aǰɪ̥vo'gadu], or [aǰvo'gadu].

Since the consonant sequences in Figure 5.2 have homologs in English, their formal pronunciation presents no difficulty to learners. What does pose a bit of a problem is the learners' initial reluctance to adopt the common pronunciation with an epenthetic /e/ or /i/, more often than not as a result of the efforts of well-meaning but misguided instructors who insist on enforcing the formal pronunciation despite the actual facts of the language.

Figure 5.2 Consonant sequences in Portuguese.

	Initial	Medial
/pt/	ptialina	rapto
/pn/	pneu	dispnéia
/ps/	psicologia	decepção
/bd/	bdélio	abdicar
/bg/	...	Abgail
/bž/	...	abjeto
/bv/	...	óbvio
/bm/	...	abmigração
/bn/	...	abnegado
/bs/	...	absorver
/tm/	tmese	atmosfera
/dg/	...	Edgar
/dv/	...	adventista
/dm/	...	admitir
/dn/	...	adnominal
/ds/	...	adstringente
/dž/	Djalma	adjunto
/kt/	ctenídeo	ectoplasma
/kn/	cnêmio	técnico
/ks/	...	ficção
/kz/	czar	eczema
/gf/	...	Agfa (a trade mark)
/gn/	gnomo	agnóstico
/ft/	ftaleína	aftose

5.5 Consonant + vowel sequences. Portuguese sequences of consonant + vowel over a word boundary are limited to four phonological possibilities, namely: (1) /n/ + vowel, (2) /r/ + vowel, (3) /l/ + vowel, (4) /s/ + vowel.

5.5.1 /n/ + vowel. The first case, /n/ + vowel, corresponds phonetically to three possible solutions, namely:

(a) nasal vowel + vowel:
la amarela /lan amaṙɛla/ [lə̃ama'ṙɛlə]

(b) nasal diphthong + vowel:
tem amigas /ten amigas/ [tẽỹa'migəs]
som agradável /son agṙadavel/ [sõw̃agṙa'davew]

(c) nasal consonantal stricture + vowel:
tem amigas /ten amigas/ [tẽỹ$^{\tilde{n}}$a'migəs]
fim alegre /fin alɛgṙe/ [fĩ$^{\tilde{n}}$a'lɛgṙi]

Problems with these sequences have to do with the articulation of a nasal consonant in final position and its linking with the following vowel, as mentioned in (4.32): tem amigas *[tẽỹmə'migəs].

5.5.2 /r̊/ + vowel. Phonological /r̊/ in final position may either be deleted altogether or surface as phonetic [r̊]. Either solution is compatible with the presence of a vowel in the following syllable, as in (5.12).

(5.12) falar isso [fa'la'isu] ~ [fa'la'r̊isu]
comer essa [ku'me'ɛsə] ~ [ku'me'r̊ɛse]

A problem often observed in the subjects' speech resulted from linking a final [x] to the following vowel, as in comer essa *[ko'me'xɛsə].

5.5.3 /l/ + vowel. Phonological /l/ in final position may surface as either phonetic [l] or [w]. In either case, there is linking with the following vowel, as in (5.13).

(5.13) papel azul [pa'pɛwa'zuw] ~ [papɛla'zuw]
tal amigo [tawa'migu] ~ [tala'migu]

The only problem observed was insistence on the articulation of final /l/ as [ɫ]. See Sections 4.3.5, 4.3.11, and 4.7.1.2.5.

5.5.4 /s/ + vowel. Final /s/ always becomes voiced when it links with a vowel in the next syllable, as in (5.14).

(5.14) rosas escuras ['r̄ɔzəzis'kurəs]
estas antigas ['ɛstazə̃'tigəs]

The only problem observed in this area was the difficulty shown by some subjects in voicing /s/. This tendency appeared stronger in those who also spoke Spanish--an understandable correlation, since in that language /s/ is not voiced in the position considered.

5.6 Postnuclear sequences. Fries (1945:18ff.) lists for English 151 postnuclear clusters, of which 65 appear in single-morpheme words and 86 result from adding a past tense morpheme (phonetically [t] or [d]), or either a plural morpheme or a third person singular morpheme (phonetically [s] or [z]). Only a few of these phonotactic possibilities have counterparts in Portuguese, but there is an important difference to consider: where English has syllable-final clusters, Portuguese has only sequences of two consonants separated by a syllable boundary, which makes the second consonant syllable-initial. Figure 5.5 shows some examples of this contrast, which presents no difficulty for learners.

Figure 5.5 Portuguese vs. English postnuclear sequences.

Portuguese		English	
/n$d/	renda	/nd/	rend
/s$t/	resto	/st/	rest
/l$d/	caldo	/ld/	cold
/m$p/	limpa	/mp/	limp
/r$d/	cardo	/rd/	card
/r$s/	curso	/rs/	curse
/r$š/	marcha	/rš/	marsh

NOTES

1. *Extraordinário* is usually [istrordi'naryu] in fast colloquial speech.
1 1 1 3 0

2. *Minas Gerais*, *Suplemento Literário*, August 28, 1976, p. 1.

3. The indefinite article is usually unstressed, hence the stress level 1 in *uma* in the examples. The two contiguous [u]'s may also be fused into a single vowel, which would yield *quero uma beladona* ['kɛrumə'bɛlə'donə].

6

PROSODY

6.1 **Introduction.** The term prosody encompasses several features which cooccur with the articulation of sound sequences, contributing to the shape of the utterance and reflecting several aspects of its communicative import. Some of those features, important as they may be, are considered to be outside the pale of linguistic study proper. For example, what is usually referred to as 'tone of voice' is actually an aggregate of phonetic features which, acting together, impart to an utterance a coloring whose communicative value lies principally in the sphere of what has been called (Leech 1974:10-27) affective and stylistic meaning. Voice quality features include deliberate drawls or lengthening of sounds, whining, extra-high or extra-low loudness, whisper, falsetto, breathy or creaky voice, intentionally clipped or syllabic pronunciation, and so on. They are created by variation in physical phenomena such as air pressure or the amplitude and vibration of the vocal cords, and they serve to signal paralinguistic elements of speech, such as the speaker's attitude, emotions, and the like. Being part and parcel of the communicative process, they are regular and collectively shared within a given linguistic community. However, they have so far proved to be rather resistant to systematic analysis and consequently, some scholars prefer to consider them paralinguistic elements of speech[1] and to reserve the label 'prosodic' for certain features of voice dynamics such as stress and pitch, which are more amenable to systematic study.[2]

6.2 **Stress.** Although it is acknowledged that 'the phonetic nature of stress remains a matter of controversy' (Sommerstein 1977:36),[3] generally speaking the term stress refers to the phonetic counterpart of the articulatory and respiratory intensity which accompanies the production of a sound. Since the articulation of any sound requires at least a minimum of such intensity, some degree of stress is always present in speech. In a given sequence of syllables, intensity varies from one syllable to another, and it is possible to detect different degrees of stress, the auditory correlate of which is loudness. It is convenient to make a distinction between stress in words considered in isolation, that is, in their citation forms (Ladefoged 1975:90), on the one hand, and stress in sequences of words such as occur in ordinary speech, on the other.

In both English and Portuguese, in the citation form of words of more than one syllable there is one syllable articulated with stronger stress than the others. For example, in words like Eng. *pivot* and Ptg. *pele*, *piv*-, and *pe*- are said to be strongly stressed, and the ultimas -*ot* and -*le* weakly stressed. It is customary, however, to say simply that the latter are unstressed and the former stressed.[4]

The position of word stress is fixed in some languages such as Czech and Hungarian, in which it falls normally on the first syllable, or Polish, in which it falls on the penult. In Portuguese, stress placement enjoys more freedom in the sense that words may be stressed on the ultima (*aqui*) or the penult (*casa*), or the antepenult (*árvore*). Stress on the fourth from last syllable is possible in compounds such as *comprávamo-los* which, while not words stricto sensu, function as such phonologically (Câmara 1970:47). In the same category are included words like *técnica* or *óbvio*, ordinarily pronounced with an epenthetic /i/ between the consonant sequences /kn/ and /bv/: ['tɛkinikə], ['ɔbiviu] (Câmara 1970:47). Except for a handful of items, however,[5] stress is fixed for a given individual word, and it plays a distinctive role, as illustrated by minimal or near-minimal pairs such as those in (6.1).

(6.1a)	sábia	sabia
	lápide	lapide
	estrídulo	estridulo
	jacá	jaca
	passará	passara

Stress position is particularly useful as a process for distinguishing between certain verb forms, as in (6.1b).

(6.1b)	1st/3rd sg. pluperfect indicative:	3rd pl. future indicative:
	falara	falará
	comera	comerá
	partira	partirá

As in Portuguese, English word stress is free in the sense that it may fall on any syllable, but it is fixed for most individual words of a given dialect.[6] Word stress is also distinctive and serves to contrast members of minimal pairs, as in (6.2a), where the items in each dyad are unrelated, or as in

(6.2b), where the phonological contrast correlates with a relationship between cognate nouns and verbs.[7]

(6.2a)	billow	below
	insight	incite
	'recap	re'cap

(6.2b)	Nouns:	Verbs:
	'contest	con'test
	'record	re'cord
	'pretest	pre'test
	'construct	con'struct
	'compound	com'pound
	'retread	re'tread

In contrast with Portuguese, English allows for variation in word stress position, in keeping with the tendency to space out stresses at regular intervals. Thus the numerals in *-teen* are normally stressed on the first syllable in counting, but on the second in an utterance like *I brought ten and she brought fif'teen*.

In English there are words with two or more stressed syllables. In *'consti,tuted* and *,consti'tution*, for example, the stronger, or primary, stress is indicated by a raised stroke ['] and the weaker, or secondary, stress is signalled by a lowered stroke [,]. Longer words may have one primary and two secondary stresses, as in *,consti'tutional,ism* or *,consub,stanti'ation*, for example.[8]

A secondary stress has been described in Portuguese for certain derived nouns and adjectives containing suffixes such as *-zal*, *-zinho*, *-inho*, and *-eiro*, as well as for adverbs in *-mente*. That accent would be somehow a reflection of the main stress of the primitive form. The following description is typical.

> Em *rapidamente* a sílaba *ra* possui um acento de intensidade menos forte que o da sílaba *men*, e se ouve mais distintamente do que as átonas existentes na palavra. Dizemos que a sílaba *men* contém o acento principal e *ra* o *acento secundário* da palavra. A sílaba em que recai o *acento secundário* chama-se, como vimos, *subtônica* (Bêchara 1972:54; italics in the original).

Examples are given in (6.3), with the primitive forms on the left and the derived ones on the right.

(6.3)	café	cafezal
	sapé	sapezeiro
	jiló	jilozinha
	jibóia	jiboinha
	lerdo	lerdamente
	calhorda	calhordamente

However, this so-called secondary stress is largely a trait of the citation forms of such words, and in ordinary speech its occurrence is limited to careful pronunciation and/or emphatic utterances. It should be noticed that the examples usually quoted involve derived forms of items in which the stressed vowel is either /ɛ/ or /ɔ/, like the examples in (6.3). In the variety of Portuguese considered here, those vowels are rare in unstressed position, and whenever they do occur their apparent prominence is due more to their phonetic quality than to the presence of a higher degree of stress. Otherwise, one would expect a secondary stress also to appear in derived forms of items in which the stressed syllable contains one of the vowels /a e i o u/, such as those exemplified in (6.4), but in fact this does not happen, unless emphasis is intended.

(6.4a)	jacá	jacazinho
	dendê	dendezinho
	saci	sacizinho
	Fulô	Fulozinha
	urubu	urubuzinho
(6.4b)	agradavel	agradavelmente
	besta	bestamente
	sofrível	sofrivelmente
	trôpego	tropegamente
	solúvel	soluvelmente

6.3 Pitch and sentence stress. The prosodic feature of pitch is the auditory correlate of frequency, that is, the rate of vibration of the vocal cords. The higher the frequency of a sound, the higher its pitch, although the proportion is not direct.[9] The pitch changes that take place throughout an utterance create a melody, or intonation contour, the analysis of which requires that one take into account the extremes of pitch variation, the relative degrees of variation between those extremes, and the direction of pitch, known as terminal contour, of a tone group. The three relevant types of terminal contours are designated by labels reminiscent of spatial metaphors, namely, rising, represented as ↑; falling, represented as ↓; and level or sustained, represented as →.[10]

Intonation patterns convey different types of information, all essential to the full communicative value of an utterance. On the one hand, intonation reveals nonlinguistic information on the speaker's attitude toward his interlocutor, or the situation in which both find themselves, or the subject of the conversation, and so forth. On the other hand, it signals the type of syntactical information which specifies whether an utterance is a statement (e.g. <u>He wants tea.</u>) or a question (e.g. <u>He wants tea?</u>), or an enumeration (e.g. <u>Tea, coffee, sugar, and milk.</u>), or an alternative (e.g. <u>Tea or coffee?</u>), and so on. Since pitch depends on frequency and the latter varies among individuals, the range of voice pitch also varies considerably from one person to another. Thus, women's and children's voices usually have far higher pitch than those of adult males, and even among individuals of the same sex and age, absolute differences in pitch, describable in terms of frequency variation, can be appreciable. Although pitch is a continuous phenomenon, linguists usually prefer to approach it by means of a system of contrasting levels. This makes it possible to describe pitch variation in terms of rises and falls from one level to another. American linguists have traditionally worked with four levels, low, medium, high, and extra-high, which are usually designated by the numbers 1, 2, 3, and 4, respectively. Because of the individual variation already referred to, these pitches are not defined in absolute terms but rather relatively to one another. Level 2, or medium, corresponds to that of the first stressed syllable in an utterance (provided that this is neither the tonic syllable nor emphatic), and it sets the norm for the other levels. Pitch rises and drops are usually described as covering one or more full levels. This is convenient for the phonological description, and the fact that it does not necessarily correspond to phonetic reality does not matter very much, since pitch ranges of less than a full level are not significant linguistically. Thus, although pitch variation takes place along a continuum, it is possible to set up, for a given language, a finite number of basic intonation patterns to describe pitch variation in full utterances.

Intonation patterns can be graphically represented in a variety of ways. In (6.5a), the spaces on a music staff, labeled from one to four, stand for four pitch levels (from lowest to highest) on which primary stresses are shown as acute accents, secondary stresses as grave accents, and weak stresses as dots; in (6.5b), pitch levels are signalled by means of superposed numbers; other possibilities include the graphic representation of a contour line superimposed on the sentence, as in (6.5e). The analysis that follows uses the system of rather iconic system of printing the syllables at different levels, as in (6.5e). In the analysis that follows, I use the system of writing out an utterance and indicating pitch levels by means of superscript and terminal contour marks placed over the appropriate stressed syllables.

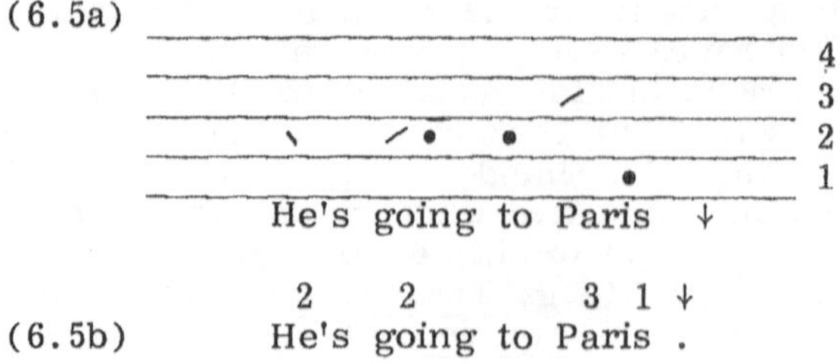

(6.5c) He's going to Paris.

(6.5d) He's going to Paris.

```
                         Pa
                           r
(6.5e)  He's go             i
             ing to          s.
```

Pitch variations are linguistically significant at the phrase and sentence level. Typically, an intonation curve cooccurs either with an entire sentence or with each of the phrases that make it up. The sequence of syllables under the same intonation curve constitutes a tonic group, and the change of pitch which contributes to make the tonic syllable more prominent is called the tonic accent.

In any given intonation contour, the tonic accent coincides with the so-called phrase stress (represented as ˝), which is the stressed syllable of the word containing the most significant bit of information in the utterance. Phrase stress is sometimes described as higher or louder than the other primary stresses in the utterance, but actually this auditory effect owes much to the combined effect of a primary stress and a change in pitch. In ordinary sentences in which no special contrast or emphasis is intended, phrase stress coincides with the last stressed syllable of the intonation contour, but this need not be so. Consider the sequence *He is there*. As an answer to the question *Where is he?*, phrase stress falls on the last word: *He is the̋re*; as a reply to the comment *He isn't there*, phrase stress may fall on the verb: *He i̋s there* (compare with the colloquial assertion *He i̋s, too*); finally, as a retort to the statement *There is no one there*, phrase stress would be on the subject: *He̋ is there*. In all of these cases, phrase stress coincides with the highest pitch in the sentence. The segment of the tonic group preceding the phrase stress is at a lower pitch level, and after the phrase stress, pitch falls steadily till the end of the utterance is reached, where pitch trails off in a falling terminal contour. This possibility of varying the place of phrase stress makes it useful as a means for highlighting any element of a sentence for purposes of emphasis or contrast. Thus, sequences like *Mary was given the potatoes* or *A Maria ganhou as batatas* can yield at least three different sentences each, implying varying intentions on the part of the speaker, and depending on whether the phrase stress falls on *potatoes*/*batatas* or *given*/*ganhou* or *Mary*/*Maria*. *She asked for pota̋toes*/*Ela pediu bata̋tas* is an ordinary, descriptive statement (as well as a possible reply to a question like *What did she ask for?*/*O que foi que ela pediu?*; it might also make explicit a contrast for the purpose of clarifying that the object requested was potatoes/batatas rather than something else. Likewise, She was gíven potatoes/ Ela gánhou batatas might imply a contrast with was sold/ comprou, or the like; finally, Shé was given potatoes/Éla ganhou batatas would contrast quite naturally with, say, But hé had to pay for them/Mas éle teve que pagá-las.[11]

6.4 **Intonation patterns.** Intonation is one of the least studied areas of Brazilian Portuguese linguistics. Except for a few short treatments, there is little available in print, and a large-scale analysis, even of a single dialect, remains a project for interested scholars. The present section deals with only a select number of basic patterns and should be considered tentative. The analysis of English intonation adopted for the contrastive analysis is based on Pike (1946), Trager and Smith (1951), and Stockwell and Bowen (1965), all of whom adopt a four-level pitch system for English. Existing analyses of Portuguese (such as Staub 1956, Rameh 1962, and Ellison et al. 1971) generally agree that a three-level pitch system suffices to describe its intonation.[12]

Pitch levels, as well as terminal contours, play a distinctive role, inasmuch as they contribute to keep apart otherwise identical utterances. However, they differ from consonants, vowels, and glides in that while these are discrete entities, pitch levels and terminal contours are not. Rather, pitch variation is continuous and its segmentation, indispensable for treating it as a series of discrete levels, can be done only indirectly, that is, in relation to the sounds which make up an utterance. Of particular relevance are the following areas of the utterance: (1) the syllables preceding the first stress; (2) the head, which is the first stressed syllable; (3) the syllable which receives phrase stress, also called the center or nucleus of the intonation contour; and (4) the syllables after the last stress.

It is a moot question whether these pitch levels and terminal contours should be considered phonemes on a par with consonants, vowels, and glides and thus treated, if only for the purposes of analysis, as discrete entities or whether they should be accorded a different treatment that would take into account their nondiscrete, essentially continuous phonetic nature.[13] For the purposes of this study, it suffices to adopt the pragmatic approach of considering them as distinctive elements in the make-up of utterances.

6.4.1 **Statement patterns: Ptg. (1) 2 1 ↓, (1) 2+ 1 ↓; Eng. (2) 3 1 ↓.** In neutral statements in Portuguese, phrase-initial unstressed syllables, if there are any, are at pitch level 1. (This is generally true of unstressed syllables in that position in all patterns.) After reaching pitch level 2 on the first stressed syllable, pitch remains at that level for the following stresses until the phrase-stressed syllable is reached, at which point there is a downward shift toward level 1. The following stressed syllables, if there are any, are also uttered below level 2. The phrase ends in a terminal contour of the falling type as the voice trails off and fades away. Examples in (6.6) illustrate this pattern, (1) 2 1 ↓.

```
          1  2          2  1    ↓
(6.6a)    O Paulo chegou ontem.

          1  2          1  1    ↓
(6.6b)    O Paulo chegou ontem.
```

The element containing the information focus is usually placed last, but syntactic constraints may determine otherwise. In (6.6a), that element is *ontem*, and the sentence offers new information as to when *Paulo's* arrival took place (as in reply to a question like *Quando o Paulo chegou?*). In (6.6b), the information focus is on the verb, regardless of whether the following adverb contains new or old information. That sentence might be used, for example, as clarification for a question such as *O que é que tem o Paulo ontem?*

There is a tendency to avoid placing too many stressed syllables in the downward part of pattern Ptg. (1) 2 1 ↓. Thus, if the information focus is on the subject, a speaker may prefer to place the latter at the end of the sentence, as in (6.6c).

```
         2             2       1      1 ↓
(6.6c) Ontem chegou um amigo meu.
```

Another declarative pattern, Ptg. (1) 2 3 1 ↓, differs from the preceding one in that the pitch of the stressed syllable of the element considered as containing the information focus is above level 2. As in the preceding pattern, pitch falls toward level 1 after the phrase-stressed syllable and the utterance ends in a falling terminal contour. The upward variation in pitch varies from a brief rise to signal mild emphasis to a full shift to level 3 to indicate strong emphasis. The difference between the two kinds of emphasis can be illustrated by the examples in (6.7a) and (6.7b).[14]

```
         1  2    2              2      2+1 ↓
(6.7a) Eu falo assim porque sou de Minas.

         1  2    2              2      3 1 ↓
(6.7b) Eu falo assim porque sou de Minas.
```

In (6.7a), the rise above level 2, but not arriving at level 3, is represented by the digit 2 followed by the plus sign (+). The speaker is underscoring a point, namely, that he was born in Minas, rather than merely providing new information;

however, there is less emphasis than in (6.7b). The latter sentence is unmistakably emphatic or contrastive, as if intended to clarify a misunderstanding, or to create a contrast with something said previously. A visually more clarifying transcription might be achieved by using dots on a staff, as in (6.7c).

(6.7c)

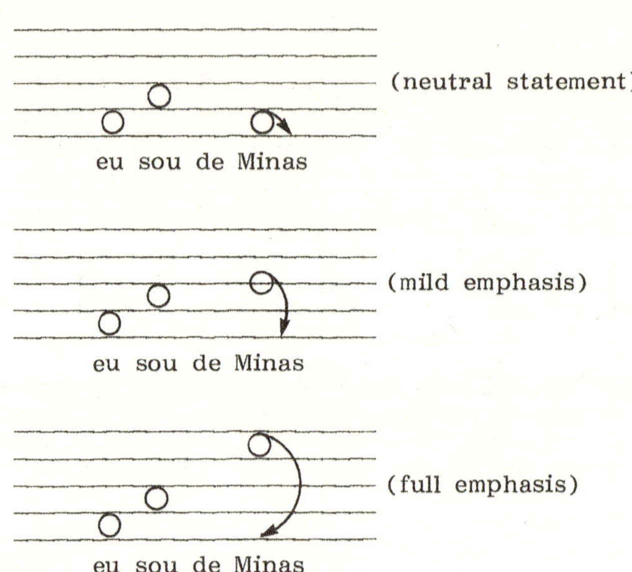

There seems to be an element of gradience in the passage from one level to another as analyzed here. The implication of this is that intermediate points between pitch levels are also important in the description of intonation, and that each of the three levels adopted here constitutes a kind of outer limit or boundary which a given variation in pitch may, but not necessarily must, reach.

In the intonation pattern typical of statements in English, pitch level 2 is reached on the first stressed syllable and remains constant on the following stresses save the last one, where it rises to pitch level 3 and then shifts downward, creating a terminal contour of the falling type.

```
        2 2      3  1 ↓
(6.8a) We live in Boulder.

         2  2      2      2  3 1 ↓
(6.8b) She worked there for two years.

        2   2   3 1 ↓
(6.8c) I'm out of work.
```

Transfer of this pattern to Portuguese invariably causes learner's utterances intended as ordinary, neutral statements to sound inappropriately emphatic or contrastive to a native speaker of Portuguese. Acquiring the correct intonation for neutral statements, however, is made difficult for the learner because the downward shift in pitch after phrase stress, typical of the pattern Ptg. (1) 2 1 ↓, corresponds in English to the intonation that signals lack of interest, boredom, or irritation on the part of the speaker, as in (6.8d).

       2   2 1   ↓
(6.8d) This is very interesting.

6.4.2 Yes/no questions: Ptg. (1) 2 2+ ↑; Eng. (1) 2 3 ↑. In a Portuguese yes/no question, the unstressed syllables before the first stress are at pitch level 1 and there is a rise to level 2 on the first stressed syllable. This level is maintained on the following stresses until the stressed syllable of the word containing the question focus is reached, whereupon pitch shifts upward without, however, fully reaching level 3. The word containing the question focus need not be the last stressed one in the utterance: if it is not, the following stressed syllables will also be uttered with pitch above level 2. The utterance ends in a rising terminal contour, as in the examples of (6.9) and (6.10).

      (1/2) 2   2+↑
(6.9) Você fala francês?

        1 1 2 2 2 2+ ↑
(6.10a) O Maurício é seu primo? (question focus on primo)

        1 1 2 2+ 2 2+ ↑
(6.10b) O Maurício é seu primo? (question focus on é)

        1 1 2+ 2+ 2+ 2+ ↑
(6.10c) O Maurício é seu primo? (question focus on Maurício)

In another pattern used with yes/no questions, the stressed syllable of the word containing the question focus is uttered at pitch level 3 or higher, and the utterance ends in a rising terminal contour, as in the examples of (6.11). This pattern signals an added connotation which may be of surprise, or incredulity, or a desire to obtain confirmation or denial of information previously provided, or just keen interest in the reply. It connotes an emphatic type of question, very different in intent from those in (6.9) and (6.10).

        1 1 2 2 2 3 ↑
(6.11a) O Maurício é seu primo?

          (1/2) 2   3 ↑
(6.11b) Você fala francês?

English yes/no questions are characterized by pitch level 3 on the last stressed syllable, followed by a terminal contour of the rising type, as in (6.12).

          (1/2) 2   3   ↑
(6.12a) Do you speak English?

          2   2   3   ↑
(6.12b) Are they coming?

          2   2   2 2   3 ↑
(6.12c) Have you got any books?

The contrast between the two languages in this case parallels the one seen in the preceding section. The difference between the two patterns, Eng. 2 3 1 ↑ and Ptg. (1) 2 2+ ↑ is a matter of degree, but the existence of pattern Ptg. (1) 2 3 ↑ suffices to make that slight difference distinctive. If the question pattern Eng. 2 3 1 ↑ is used in Portuguese, it will be interpreted as signalling either a degree of insistence not present in ordinary yes/no questions or the intention to contrast or emphasize the sentence element containing the question focus, as in (6.13).

          2   3 ↑
(6.13a) Eles vêm? (I'm getting tired of waiting for them!)

          (1/2) 2   3 ↑
(6.13b) Você tem a chave? (Or did you forget to bring it again?)

6.4.3 Questions with interrogative words: Ptg. 1 2 1 ↓; Eng. 2 3 1 ↓. In English, this type of question is characterized by an intonation contour very similar to that of statements (cf. 6.8), as shown in (6.14).

          2   3   1 1 ↓
(6.14a) How much is it?

          2   3 1   ↓
(6.14b) Where is the library?

          2 2   2   3 1 ↓
(6.14c) Why don't you say it?

In Portuguese, the tendency is to pronounce the interrogative word at a higher pitch than the ensuing stressed syllables. That pitch is usually at level 2 for ordinary questions, and higher if emphasis is intended. After the interrogative word, pitch falls steadily toward level 1. The utterance may end in a falling terminal contour in neutral, impersonal questions, as in (6.15), or in a short rising terminal contour, which indicates an attitude of interest or cordiality on the part of the speaker, as in (6.16).

```
          2 1     1       1↓
(6.15a) Quando você chegou?

          1 2     1   1  1↓
(6.15b) Quedê o seu carro?

        2       1         1   ↑
(6.15c) Onde  é a biblioteca?

          2       1       1↑
(6.16a) Quando você chegou?

            2     1         1   ↑
(6.16b) Quedê a sua namorada?

         2     1  1  1   ↑
(6.16c) Como se faz isso?
```

If transferred to Portuguese, the pattern Eng. 2 3 1 ↓ exemplified in (6.14) tends to make utterances sound like emphatic statements, as in (6.17).

```
            2     2         3  1↓
(6.17a) Quedê a sua namorada?

         2        2  3  1↓
(6.17b) Como se faz isso?
```

6.4.4 Greetings: Ptg. 2 1 ↓, 2 2 ↓, 1 2 1 ↓, 2 3 1 ↓; Eng. 2 3 1 ↓, 2 3 1 ↑. Several intonation patterns are possible in Portuguese for greetings. A somewhat formal (though not necessarily unfriendly) pattern has pitch level 2 on the first stressed syllable, after which there is a fall toward pitch level 1 and a falling terminal contour, as shown in (6.18). Both this type of descending intonation and the patterns shown in (6.19), with pitch level 2 constant up to the last stressed syllable, signal routine greetings. A more cheerful connotation is conveyed by a rise in pitch level, from the first to the last stressed syllable, followed by falling final contour, as in (6.20).

```
        2    1↓
(6.18) Bom dia.

        2    2↓
(6.19) Bom dia.
```

1 2 ↓
(6.20a) Boa tarde.

2 3 1↓
(6.20b) Boa noite.

1 2 1↓
(6.20c) Até logo.

Several patterns are also possible in English, as shown in (6.21) and (6.22).

2 3 1 ↓
(6.21a) Good evening.

2 3 1 ↓
(6.21b) Good morning.

2 3 ↑
(6.22a) Good night.

2 3 1 ↑
(6.22b) See you tomorrow.

2 3 2 ↑
(6.22c) See you later.

Falling or sustained terminal contours, as in (6.21), are usually associated with perfunctory or indifferent greetings, whereas rising terminal contours, as in (6.22), signal a higher degree of cordiality or cheerfulness. This is possibly why learners tend to be reluctant to use falling contours with greetings such as those in (6.18)-(6.20). However, transfer of rising final contour to Portuguese produces greetings which sound over-cheerful, if not tinged with obsequiousness, or at any rate too lively for ordinary circumstances.[15]

6.4.5 Contrastive statements: Ptg. (1) 2 3 1 ↓; Eng. (1) 2 4 1 ↓. In both languages, the intonation of contrastive statements involves a change in pitch on the stressed syllable of the word which constitutes a contrast focus. In English sentences like those in (6.23), the item Mary contains new information, part of which is its contrastiveness in relation to Peter, which presumably contains old information. The same considerations are valid for textiles and furniture, respectively (6.24). In either case, contrastiveness of the new items is indicated by a rise in pitch to level 4, followed by a fall to level 1 and falling terminal contour. Each sentence includes two intonation contours, both of the falling type.

```
        2     2       3 1 ↓ 2  2          4 1↓
(6.23) I didn't talk to Peter, I talked to Mary.

         2      2       3   1     ↓  2    2      4  1  ↓
(6.24) We don't handle furniture, we handle textiles.
```

In Portuguese, contrastiveness likewise involves an upward shift in pitch, although only to level 3, as shown in (6.25) and (6.26).

```
                  2          3   1    2             3  1
(6.25) Eu não falei com o Pedro, falei com a Marta.

         2            2          31        2            3  1
(6.26) Nós não vendemos mobília, vendemos tecidos.
```

Since in Portuguese pitch levels above 3 are used primarily for emphasis, transfer of the English pattern causes an ordinary contrastive sentence to convey far more intensity of feeling than intended by the speaker.

6.4.6 Sequences: Ptg. (1) 2 → 2 → 1 ↓, (1) 2 ↑, 2 ↑, 1 ↓; Eng. (2) 3 → 3 → 3 1 ↓; 2 ↑ 2 ↑ 3 1 ↓. In both languages, sequences of coordinated items--as in lists or enumerations--are characterized by either rising or sustained pitch contours after each item of the series but the last one. When the last item is reached, the end of the series is signalled by a shift in pitch. This shift is downward in Portuguese, from level 2 to level 1, and fading into a falling terminal contour, as in (6.27). In English, pitch shifts upward to level 3 on the stressed syllable, and then downward to level 1, and thence to a falling terminal contour, as in (6.28).

```
          1  2 →   2 →   2     →  1    1↓
(6.27a) Arroz, feijão, açúcar e carne.

          2 ↑    2 ↑   2 ↑    2    ↑  1    ↓
(6.27b) Um, dois, três, quatro, cinco.

           3 →    3    →    3   → 2     3 1↓
(6.28a) Rice, beans, sugar, and meat.

           2  ↑  2 ↑    2   ↑  2   ↑  3 1↓
(6.28b) One, two, three, four, five.
```

Two contrasts are apparent regarding sequences. First, use of pitch level 3, as in (6.28a), would signal in Portuguese some kind of emphasis normally absent in ordinary enumeration. Second, there is the shift of pitch level on the stressed syllable of the last item. Whereas in Portuguese pitch falls toward level 1, in English it rises to level 3 and only then falls toward level 1. If transferred to Portuguese, this intonation would signal emphasis or contrast, such as might be caused by finding an unexpected item in a series, as in (6.29).

```
        1  2 →   2 →  2   →    3 1↓
(6.29) Arroz, feijão, açúcar e baratas!
```

NOTES

1. On prosodic vs. paralinguistic elements of speech, see Crystal and Quirk (1964) and Crystal (1969:128ff.).

2. Features of voice dynamics 'are under the speaker's control, and therefore can be acquired; consequently they tend to be copied from other people, and so are capable of characterizing social groups as well as individuals' (Abercrombie 1967:95).

3. Concerning analysis of stress, see Crystal (1969), Ladefoged (1975), Lehiste (1970), and O'Connor (1973).

4. The role of subphonological levels of stress is mentioned in Section 5.2.

5. Exceptions include doublets like projétil/projetil (pl. projéteis/projetis) or ruim [r̄u'ĩ]/[r̄ũỹ] and pairs in which a standard form alternates with a popular variant, e.g. rubrica vs. rúbrica (pop.), crisântemo vs. crisantemo (pop.), filantropo vs. filântropo (pop.), boêmia vs. boemia (pop.), and so on.

6. Doublets include ciga'rette vs. 'cigarette, con'tractor vs. 'contractor, con'verse vs. 'converse, con'trite vs. 'contrite, the numerals in -teen (e.g. 'thirteen vs. thir'teen), and so on.

7. See Householder (1971:Chapter 14) for a detailed study of these lexical items.

8. According to Ladefoged (1975:99ff.), the difference between primary and secondary stress is due to other prosodic phenomena, such as intonation, and it is possible to analyze English syllables simply as either stressed or unstressed. (For a critique, see Hill 1977). However, the contrast primary vs. secondary stress has traditionally been accepted in English phonology, particularly with regard to American English, and furthermore it is a useful one for contrastive analysis, for which reasons it is retained here.

9. See Crystal (1969:108ff.) for a discussion of pitch and frequency.

10. On the spatial metaphors (and others) used for describing pitch variation, see Abercrombie (1967:103).

11. Beyond the scope of a contrastive phonological analysis is the fact that displacement of phrase stress may be superseded by other formal devices, such as word order, for highlighting or contrasting purposes in Portuguese.

12. A fourth level (extra high) may be needed, however, to account for very emphatic pitch.

13. Some authors would exclude pitch from phonology altogether: 'To the extent that intonational features are continuously variable ... phonology ... [has] nothing to say about them. Phonology imposes discrete categorization on continuous sound ... intonation ... maps certain continuously variable aspects of reality (largely relating to the speaker's attitudes) into continuously variable aspects of sound, bypassing, as it were, all discrete structure' (Sommerstein 1977:39). The analysis of pitch in terms of phonemic levels has been criticized by Bolinger (1958), in favor of an analysis based on melodic contours of intonation. Regarding this position, Lehiste (1970:96) suggests that 'in spite of the apparent mutual exclusiveness of the two points of view, it nevertheless appears probable that both levels and configurations have to be specified for certain purposes'.

14. The notation (1/2) used in (6.7a) and elsewhere indicates that an item can be uttered at either pitch level 1 or 2. This variation results from the possibility of unstressing certain words, such as subject pronouns, possessives, auxiliary verbs, and the like.

15. Some informants have reacted differently to Portuguese greetings uttered with rising terminal contours. In the case of male voices, four informants (two men and two women) agreed that the rising terminal contour created an impression of effeminacy and, in the case of feminine voices, of excessive cheerfulness or overemphasis.

REFERENCES

Abercrombie, David. 1967. Elements of general phonetics. Edinburgh: Edinburgh University Press.

Agard, Frederick B. 1969. Pronúncia e ortografia do inglês para falantes de espanhol e português. In: O Simpósio de São Paulo. Atas do Programa Interamericano de Lingüística e Ensino de Idiomas (PILEI). São Paulo: Faculdade de Filosofia, Letras e Ciências Humanas da Universidade de São Paulo. 201-209.

Agard, Frederick B. 1970. Prelegeri de analiză contrastiva. Bucharești: Centrul de multiplicare al Universității din Bucuresti.

Agard, Frederick B., and Robert J. Di Pietro. 1965. The sounds of English and Italian. Chicago: University of Chicago Press.

Almeida, António. 1976. The Portuguese nasal vowels: Phonetics and phonemics. In: Readings in Portuguese linguistics. Edited by Jürgen Schmidt-Radefeldt. Amsterdam: North-Holland. 348-396.

Amaral, Amadeu. 1920. O dialecto caipira. São Paulo: Casa Editora 'O Livro'.

Back, Eurico. 1973. São fonemas as vogais nasais do português? Construtura 4. 297-317.

Barbosa, Jorge Morais. 1962. Les voyelles nasales portugaises: Interprétation phonologique. In: Proceedings of the Fourth International Congress of Phonetic Sciences, Helsinki, 1961. The Hague: Mouton. 691-708.

Bechara, Evanildo. 1972. Moderna gramática portuguesa. Curso de 1° e 2° graus. 19th ed. São Paulo: Companhia Editora Nacional.

Bolinger, Dwight. 1958. A theory of pitch accent in English. Word 14.109-149.

Bolinger, Dwight. 1975. Aspects of language. 2nd ed. New York: Harcourt Brace Jovanovich.

Câmara, Joaquim Mattoso, Jr. 1953. Para o estudo da fonêmica portuguesa. Rio de Janeiro: Organização Simões.

Câmara, Joaquim Mattoso, Jr. 1968. 'Muta cum muta' in Portuguese? Word 24.286-289.

Câmara, Joaquim Mattoso, Jr. 1969. Problemas de lingüística descritiva. Petrópolis: Editora Vozes Limitada.

Câmara, Joaquim Mattoso, Jr. 1970. Estrutura da língua portuguesa. Petrópolis: Editora Vozes Limitada.

Câmara, Joaquim Mattoso, Jr. 1972. The Portuguese language. Translated by Anthony J. Naro. Chicago: University of Chicago Press.

Chomsky, Noam, and Morris Halle. 1968. The sound pattern of English. New York: Harper and Row.

Cintra, Geraldo. 1962. Ensaios sôbre a estrutura do português do Brasil. Estudos 1.1:17-31; 1.3:19-31; 1.4:15-25.

Cintra, Geraldo. 1978. Entropia silábica do português. Dissertation for the degree of Mestre em Ciências da Comunicação, Escola de Comunicações e Artes, Universidade de São Paulo.

Corder, S. Pit. 1967. The significance of learners errors. International Review of Applied Linguistics 5.4:161-170.

Corder, S. Pit. 1971. Idiosyncratic dialects and error analysis. International Review of Applied Linguistics 9.2: 147-160.

Corder, S. Pit. 1973. Introducing applied linguistics. Harmondsworth, England: Penguin.

Corder, S. Pit. 1975. The language of second-language learners: The broad issues. Modern Language Journal 59.8:409-413.

Cressey, William W. 1978. Spanish phonology and morphology: A generative view. Washington, D.C.: Georgetown University Press.

Crystal, David. 1969. Prosodic systems and intonation in English. Cambridge: Cambridge University Press.

Crystal, David, and Randolph Quirk. 1964. Systems of prosodic and paralinguistic features in English. The Hague: Mouton.

Delattre, Pierre. 1965. Comparing the phonetic features of English, French, German and Spanish: An interim report. Heidelberg: Julius Groos Verlag.

Delattre, Pierre. 1966. Voyelles diphtonguées et voyelles pures. In: Studies in French and comparative phonetics. The Hague: Mouton. (First published in The French Review 37 [October 1963]. 64-76.)

Ellison, Fred P., et al. 1971. Modern Portuguese. New York: Alfred A. Knopf.

Feldman, David. 1967. A comparison of the segmental phonemes of Brazilian Portuguese and American Spanish. Linguistics 29.44-57.

Fries, Charles C. 1945. Teaching and learning English as a foreign language. Ann Arbor: University of Michigan Press.

Gomes de Matos, Francisco. 1970. A note on vowel fusion in Brazilian Portuguese. Hispania 53.1:80-82.

Hall, Robert A., Jr. 1943. The unit phonemes of Brazilian Portuguese. Studies in Linguistics 1.15:1-6.

Hanzeli, Victor E. 1975. Learner's language: Implications of recent research for foreign language instruction. Modern Language Journal 59.8:426-432.

Harris, James W. 1969. Spanish phonology. Research Monograph No. 54. Cambridge, Mass.: MIT Press.

Head, Brian F. 1964. A comparison of the segmental phonology of Lisbon and Rio de Janeiro. Ph.D. dissertation. University of Texas.

Hensey, F. 1968. Questões de fonologia gerativa: As regras de pluralização. Estudos lingüísticos 3.1-2:1-10.

Hensey, F. 1972. The sociolinguistics of the Brazilian-Uruguayan border. The Hague: Mouton.

Hill, Archibald A. 1958. Introduction to linguistic structures. From sound to sentence in English. New York: Harcourt, Brace.

Hill, Kenneth C. 1977. Review of: Ladefoged (1975). Language 53.4:911-917.

Hooper, Joan B. 1976. An introduction to natural generative phonology. New York: Academic Press.

Houaiss, Antônio. 1959. Tentativa de descrição do sistema vocálico do português culto na área dita carioca. Rio de Janeiro: Departamento de Imprensa Nacional.

Householder, Fred W. 1971. Accent, stress, prosodies, and tonal features. In: Linguistic speculations. Cambridge: Cambridge University Press.

Istre, Giles L. 1971. A phonological analysis of a Brazilian Portuguese interior dialect. Ph.D. dissertation. Louisiana State University and Agricultural and Mechanical College.

Istre, Giles L. 1975. An examination of Portuguese nasal occlusives. Revista Brasileira de Lingüística 2.2:20-32.

James, Carl. 1971. The exculpation of contrastive linguistics. In: Papers in contrastive linguistics. Edited by Gerhard Nickel. Cambridge: Cambridge University Press. 53-68.

Jones, Daniel. 1956. An outline of English phonetics. 8th ed. Cambridge, England: Heffer.

Kohler, K. 1971. On the adequacy of phonological theories for contrastive studies. In: Papers in contrastive linguistics. Edited by Gerhard Nickel. Cambridge: Cambridge University Press, 83-88.

Kufner, Herbert L. 1971. Kontrastive Phonologie Deutsch-Englisch. Stuttgart: Ernst Klett Verlag.

Kurath, Hans. 1964. A phonology and prosody of modern English. Ann Arbor: The University of Michigan Press.

Ladefoged, Peter. 1975. A course in phonetics. New York: Harcourt Brace Jovanovich.

Lado, Robert. 1968. Contrastive linguistics in a mentalistic theory of language learning. In: Georgetown University

Round Table on Languages and Linguistics 1968. Edited by James E. Alatis. Washington, D.C.: Georgetown University Press. 123-135.

Lee, W. R. 1968. Thoughts on contrastive linguistics in the context of language teaching. In: Georgetown University Round Table on Languages and Linguistics 1968. Edited by James E. Alatis. Washington, D.C.: Georgetown University Press. 185-194.

Leech, Geoffrey. 1974. Semantics. Harmondsworth, England: Penguin.

Lehiste, Ilse. 1970. Suprasegmentals. Cambridge, Mass.: MIT Press.

Mascherpe, Mário. 1970. Análise comparativa dos sistemas fonológicos do inglês e do português. Assis (São Paulo): Cadeira de Língua e Líteratura Inglesa, Faculdade de Filosofia, Ciências e Letras de Assis.

Mateus, Maria Helena Mira. 1975. Aspectos da fonologia portuguesa. Lisbon: Publicação do Centro de Estudos Filológicos.

Moulton, William G. 1962. The sounds of English and German. Chicago: University of Chicago Press.

Nemser, William. 1971. Approximate systems of foreign language learners. International Review of Applied Linguistics 9.2:115-123.

Nobiling, Oskar. 1903. As vogais nasais em português. Translated by Dinah Maria Isensee Callou and Maria Helena Duarte Marques. Littera, No. 12 (September-December 1974). 79-109. (Originally published as Die Nasalvokale im Portugiesischen. Die Neueren Sprachen 11.129-153.)

O'Connor, J. D. 1973. Phonetics. Harmondsworth, England: Penguin.

Pike, Kenneth. 1946. The intonation of American English. Ann Arbor: University of Michigan Press.

Pottier, Bernard. 1967. Alternances vocaliques et zones phonémiques. In: Estudos Filológicos. (Homenagem a Serafim da Silva Neto.) Edited by Leodegário A. de Azevedo Filho. Rio de Janeiro: Edições Tempo Brasileiro.

Rameh, Cléa A. S. 1962. Contrastive analysis of English and Portuguese intonation. M.S. dissertation No. 2118. Georgetown University.

Reed, David W., and Yolanda Leite. 1947 [1943]. The segmental phonemes of Brazilian Portuguese: Standard Paulista dialect. In: Phonemics: A technique for reducing languages to writing. By Kenneth L. Pike. Ann Arbor: University of Michigan Press. 194-202.

Rodrigues, Ada Natal. 1974. A dialeto caipira na região de Piracicaba. São Paulo: Editora Ática S.A.

Schane, Sanford A. 1971. The phoneme revisited. Language 47.3:503-521.

Selinker, Larry. 1972. Interlanguage. International Review of Applied Linguistics 10.3:209-231.

Sloat, Clarence, Sharon Henderson Taylor, and James E. Hoard. 1978. Introduction to phonology. Englewood Cliffs, N.J.: Prentice-Hall.

Sommerstein, Alan H. 1977. Modern phonology. London: Edward Arnold.

Staub, Augustine. 1956. Comparative study of English and Portuguese intonation. M.S. dissertation No. 1354. Georgetown University.

Stockwell, Robert P., and J. Donald Bowen. 1965. The sounds of English and Spanish. Chicago: University of Chicago Press.

Terrell, Tracy D., and Maruxa Salgués de Cargill. 1979. Lingüística aplicada a la enseñanza del español a anglohablantes. New York: John Wiley and Sons.

Trager, George L., and Henry Lee Smith, Jr. 1951. An outline of English structure. Norman, Okla.: Battenburg Press.

Vandresen, Paulino. 1974. O vocalismo português: Implicações teóricas. Revista Brasileira de Lingüística 1.1:80-103.

Venneman, Theo. 1974a. Phonological concreteness in natural generative grammar. In: Toward tomorrow's linguistics. Edited by R. Shuy and C.-J. Bailey. Washington, D.C.: Georgetown University Press.

Venneman, Theo. 1974b. Words and syllables in natural generative grammar. Natural Phonology Parasession. Chicago: Chicago Linguistic Society. 346-374.

Wang, William S-Y. 1968. Vowel features, paired variables, and the English vowel shift. Language 44.695-708.

Wardhaugh, Ronald. 1970. The contrastive analysis hypothesis. TESOL Quarterly 4.123-130.

Wise, Claude Merton. 1957. Applied phonetics. Chapter 25: Brazilian Portuguese dialect. Englewood Cliffs, N.J.: Prentice-Hall. 512-532.

www.ingramcontent.com/pod-product-compliance
Lightning Source LLC
LaVergne TN
LVHW090810070826
844660LV00022B/1135

* 9 7 8 0 8 7 8 4 0 0 8 2 9 *